Rhetorical Public Speaking

This textbook offers an innovative approach to public speaking by employing the rhetorical canon as a means of constructing artful speech in a multi-mediated environment.

By stressing how contemporary public speaking continues the classical art of persuasion, this book provides a foundation to guide students in constructing and delivering messages that address matters of concern and interest to their audience. This edition features contemporary as well as historical examples to highlight key concepts and show how rhetoric works in practice. It not only emphasizes the traditional skills of face-to-face oratory, but it also includes a chapter solely dedicated to highlighting the techniques and tactics of digital social influencing that adapts public speaking to online platforms. Each chapter includes speech excerpts, summaries, and exercises for review and retention.

This textbook for courses in public speaking and rhetoric will particularly appeal to instructors wishing to foreground speaking as engaged citizens on public and political issues.

Online resources include an instructor's manual with discussion and test questions, video links, and sample materials.

Nathan Crick is a Professor in the Department of Communication at Texas A&M University. He is the author of seven books, including *Dewey for a New Age of Fascism: Teaching Democratic Habits*; *Rhetoric and Power: The Drama of Classical Greece*; *Democracy and Rhetoric: John Dewey on the Arts of Becoming*; and *The Keys of Power: The Rhetoric and Politics of Transcendentalism*.

"Like a good parallel construction, which students will learn about in this book, *Rhetorical Public Speaking* admirably balances two important objectives. While it makes the rhetorical tradition accessible to modern students, it also demonstrates the enduring practical value of the liberal arts for the digital age. From classical speech genres to new media situations, the text illustrates the perennial adaptability of a rhetorical education."

John J. Jasso, *Ave Maria University, USA*

"*Rhetorical Public Speaking* is simply the best public speaking textbook I have ever read. It is sufficiently comprehensive without being overwhelming or needlessly technical. It uses a range of examples and explanations more relevant to contemporary college students than those found in other books. *Rhetorical Public Speaking* is the first textbook of its kind that I would enthusiastically recommend, and I expect it to become one of the most widely used public speaking textbooks at the college level for many years to come."

Calum Matheson, *University of Pittsburgh, USA*

"Simultaneously an incisive public speaking handbook and a cogent primer on the rhetorical tradition, this lively and thoughtful text teaches students not only how to speak, but why we speak. It is a manual for teaching students to become both artistic producers of and thoughtful, engaged audiences for public discourse in an ever-shifting media environment."

Nicholas L. Stefanski, *Alfred State College, USA*

Praise for the third edition:

"A thoughtful, methodical and inspiring handbook that shows students how to become engaged citizens by means of the spoken word, that is, eloquent transgressors of silence and public apathy."

John Poulakos, *University of Pittsburgh, USA*

Rhetorical Public Speaking

Social Influence in the Digital Age

Fourth Edition

Nathan Crick

Routledge
Taylor & Francis Group

NEW YORK AND LONDON

Cover image: fizkes/Getty; FatCamera/Getty

Fourth edition published
by Routledge
605 Third Avenue, New York, NY 10158

and by Routledge
4 Park Square, Milton Park, Abingdon, Oxon OX14 4RN

Routledge is an imprint of the Taylor & Francis Group, an informa business

[First edition published by Pearson Education, Inc 2011]
[Third edition published by Routledge 2017]

Library of Congress Cataloging-in-Publication Data
Names: Crick, Nathan, author.
Title: Rhetorical public speaking : social influence in the digital age /
Nathan Crick.
Description: Fourth edition. | New York, NY : Routledge, 2023. |
Includes bibliographical references and index. |
Identifiers: LCCN 2022019239 (print) | LCCN 2022019240 (ebook) |
ISBN 9781032289847 (paperback) | ISBN 9781032328003 (hardback) |
ISBN 9781003316787 (ebook)
Subjects: LCSH: Public speaking.
Classification: LCC PN4121 .C745 2023 (print) |
LCC PN4121 (ebook) | DDC 808.5/1--dc23/eng/20220607
LC record available at https://lccn.loc.gov/2022019239
LC ebook record available at https://lccn.loc.gov/2022019240

ISBN: 978-1-032-32800-3 (hbk)
ISBN: 978-1-032-28984-7 (pbk)
ISBN: 978-1-003-31678-7 (ebk)

DOI: 10.4324/9781003316787

Typeset in Bembo
by Taylor & Francis Books

Access the Support Material: www.Routledge.com/9781032289847

Contents

Preface

The purpose of this book is to give students a practical understanding of how public speaking can function as a **rhetorical intervention**—as an act of persuasion designed to alter how other people think about and respond to public affairs that affect their lives. The audience for this book is the **engaged citizen**: that individual who is an active participant in the democratic process of debate, deliberation, and persuasion as it relates to issues of public concern. However, in today's multimedia environment, there are many types of engaged citizen. Consequently, this book distinguishes between two genres of public speaking available to those who wish to make an impact on others. First, **rhetorical public speaking** focuses on techniques of face-to-face oral performance that bring people together in a shared space to deliberate about matters of common concerns. Second, **digital social influencing** focuses on techniques of video recording, editing, and dissemination by which individuals create online followings based on shared interests. This book addresses both genres of public speaking in order to address the widest possible scope of persuasion that can help engaged citizens to pursue civic engagement in a digital age.

Features of This Edition

This fourth edition has been updated and expanded to provide students with the tools they need to be effective public speakers. The following are key features of the text:

- A new chapter focused exclusively on the techniques of digital social influencing for use in teaching courses designed to master recording and editing techniques.
- A comprehensive and consecutive presentation of the five canons of rhetoric that allows you to efficiently master the basics of rhetoric in the first few weeks of class.
- Lists of discussion questions and class exercises at the end of each chapter developed over two decades of teaching public speaking.
- A consistent stress on the rhetorical aspect of public speaking that focuses attention on the needs of the audience and the relationship between a speech and a rhetorical situation.
- New sections discussing stasis theory, narrative composition, social influencing, memory palace, and fallacies.
- A streamlined text that simplifies concepts and reduces chapter numbers and length that conforms to a fifteen-week course in public speaking for high school and college students.
- An emphasis on ethos, pathos, and logos as distinct forms of proof that draw from classical insights but enrich them with contemporary rhetorical theory.

1 Rhetorical Public Speaking

Rhetorical public speaking remains versatile and powerful in the digital age. The proliferation of digital platforms has not led to a reduction in the importance of public speaking; it has led to its ever-increasing centrality to our political and social lives. To be sure, the age of the crowded city filled with street-corner orators is gone. But the power of the art remains. We are more exposed than ever to rhetorical performances through digital communication technologies, which in turn have provided an efficient means of gathering people together in a shared space to experience traditional oratory. And even if the quantity of public speaking has declined, its transformative potential has only increased. Digital social influencing and rhetorical public speaking are not competitors; they are counterparts. And they are both applications of the art of rhetoric.

I focus on the *rhetorical* aspect of public speaking to emphasize its situated, strategic, and pragmatic aspects. Too often, public speaking is defined simply as the act of speaking itself, quite apart from its purpose or occasion. Such a definition tends to focus on the intentions and actions of the speaker to the neglect of the needs and desires of an audience. By contrast, describing public speaking as *rhetorical* highlights the way in which our speech provides a fitting response to some present problem (its situated character), employs conscious persuasive means to transform the way an audience thinks, feels, and behaves (its strategic character), for the purpose of changing the situation for the better (its pragmatic character). In sum, **rhetoric** is *the persuasive art of addressing pressing public concerns before a public audience in order to transform some aspect of a problematic situation by encouraging new forms of thought and action.* Let us break this definition into its parts:

1   *The persuasive art*: Referring to rhetoric as a persuasive art distinguishes it from a mere instinctual or unreflective talent. *Art* thus does not mean an intuitive creativity or genius lacking in method. Quite the opposite, art requires the application of rational concepts and methods in the creative process of inventing means of changing people's ideas, transforming their attitudes, and arousing their emotions.

DOI: 10.4324/9781003316787-1

2 Rhetorical Public Speaking

2 *of addressing pressing public concerns*: Except for matters of idle curiosity, the only reason we voluntarily expose ourselves to rhetorical discourse is because it speaks to a shared concern that is in the forefront of our consciousness. We listen to rhetoric with the hope that the person speaking might be able to suggest a path out of our current predicament or achieve an aim that may have eluded us.

3 *before a public audience*: The *public* character of the audience means that it addresses an audience of relative strangers who come together to address areas of common concern. Persuading an audience of friends may still employ rhetoric, but that rhetoric generally appeals to the unique bonds of those friends rather than their shared characteristics as part of a larger public.

4 *in order to transform some aspect of a problematic situation*: Rhetoric seeks to change some aspect of the natural or social environment that is *felt* to be problematic by a public audience. This shared experience of uncertainty, anxiety, and urgency focuses people's attention on a speech and thus gives it a unique power.

5 *by encouraging new forms of thought and action*: The means by which rhetoric transforms that environment is by the use of symbols which encourage other people to change their attitudes toward objective things in the world. Rhetoric is thus an indirect form of action. It makes changes by changing what people think and feel so that they might act differently and thereby resolve some problem or achieve some goal.

Today, rhetoric has become virtually ever-present in our lives. Anyone with access to social media has the ability to act rhetorically virtually at any moment in the day. In our social lives we swim through a constant flood of opinions, arguments, appeals, and persuasion that arises in response to current events as individuals seek to make some impact on opinion. Rhetoric as defined this way is not tied to any one form of expression. Rhetoric was originally connected with oratory but quickly found expression in written pamphlets, letters, and books. Today, people use rhetorical techniques in video, photography, memes, movies, posters, tweets, texts, music, and advertisements. Rhetorical techniques can be adapted to any medium.

This book will distinguish between two genres of rhetoric. First, **rhetorical public speaking** designates a traditional face-to-face speech performance before a live audience that seeks to transform a collection of individual hearers into a common and committed audience through the power of the spoken word. What sets public speaking apart from other mediated forms of communication, such as writing or video, is the simple fact of being in the same place at the same time. This sharing of direct experience can make public speaking a very powerful medium. This is because, as Walter Ong has pointed out, "spoken words are always modification of a total, existential situation, which always engages the body."[1] When we watch someone on a screen or read his or her words on paper, we can easily get distracted and turn our attention to other things; but when we are present together to listen to a speech that captures our attention, we can commit ourselves completely to the experience of being together in a shared space. Despite our ability to communicate through media as never before, there is a very basic need in every human being for intimate human contact that comes from simply being with others in the same place at the same time and recognizing and welcoming one another's presence. We may not speak to one another in person as much as we had in the past, but that only means that we must be prepared to do so with passion and with power when the moment calls.

Second, **digital social influencing** refers to how social influence is communicated on digital platforms. If traditional rhetoric often stressed the clash of opinions and the need to confront opposition, social influencing tends to emphasize advice, conformity, socialization, peer pressure, leadership, support, growth, and encouragement. **Social influencing** refers to the process by which an individual's attitudes, beliefs or behavior are modified by the presence or action of others to meet the demands of a social environment. Whereas rhetorical public speaking continues the oratorical traditions of the classical world, digital social influencing introduces new strategies adapted to meet the needs of the contemporary global village. Whereas the art of rhetoric originated in the realm of law and politics and stressed how language could meet the pressing needs of justice and deliberation, social influencing grew out of the proliferation of social media that gathers like-minded followers who share the same interests. Both are rhetorical, but in different ways. The next chapter will discuss digital social influencing. This introductory chapter, however, will focus on rhetorical public speaking in order to connect more closely with the classical tradition.

The art of rhetoric developed with the purpose of crafting a public speech that functioned as a shared event with a past and a future. Even a speech that is videotaped and rebroadcast is not the same as the speech heard by those physically present. The speech includes all the events that led up to it (including the travel required for people to reach the same place, the time it takes to gather together and to wait, and any preceding events that introduced it) and the actions that follow it (including conversation with others about the speech, any proceeding events, and the final departure of the guests). The public speech is not separate from its history. It requires its history to be meaningful. Those who watch a speech on television may remember certain words or phrases used, and perhaps an image of the audience flashed before the screen, but their memory of watching the speech is tied up with the physical context of where it is watched—a living

---

1   Walter Ong, *Orality and Literacy: The Technologizing of the Word* (New York: Routledge, 2002), 67.

room, a bar, a classroom, and the like. For the people actually present, however, the speech is an event that is a part of a larger drama, even if it includes merely the conversation with co-workers before and after a boardroom meeting.

The unique thing about public speaking is not the content or even the style of the words; it is the fact that the words are spoken in the company of others in a common, shared space. When we speak, we are not just conveying information; we are forming relationships between ourselves and the audience, the audience members with each other, and everyone with the total environmental context. With each word spoken, one must manage a delicate process of adjusting to constant **feedback**, which is the return messages that are constantly being sent by the other people involved in the communicative process. Being present at an oral performance is a whole-body experience that we feel "in touch with" in a way that cannot compare to the experience of watching the same speech on a video recording. This almost intangible quality is more easily experienced than explained. It is the difference between being part of a graduation ceremony and receiving the diploma in the mail, between going to a place of worship to hear a sermon and reading a religious text at home, between making a toast at a wedding and sending a card of congratulations, between hearing an inspirational speech before a big game and receiving an email of that speech, or between announcing the birth of a child before one's family at Thanksgiving and distributing a video of that speech online.

The Canons of Rhetoric

Despite changes in the technology and culture of communication, the aims of rhetoric have remained impressively stable. In the ancient Roman Republic, the eloquent senator Cicero codified the three aims of oratory, which in Latin he called *docere, delectare*, and *movere*. **Docere** means to teach or to instruct an audience in a way that makes them understand and come to accept certain ideas or principles as true and valuable. This is accomplished through careful reasoning and the reliance on established principles, clear proofs, and reliable causes. **Delectare** means to delight and to please an audience in a way that makes the experience of oratory pleasurable to hear and to witness as a performance. This is accomplished by attention to the sound and imagery of words that imitated the figures of poetry in a way that appealed to a public ear. **Movere** means to move an audience by arousing and directing emotions in a way that encourages specific attitudes and actions. This is accomplished by dramatic narratives, concrete examples, and vivid imagery that made people feel react viscerally to the people, objects, and events around them. Cicero's advice remains as valuable as ever. Every act of persuasion always involves each of these actions to some degree, if only because human beings will always crave experiences that satisfy curiosity, please the senses, and evoke passion.

Similarly, the **means of persuasion** by which a speaker can teach, delight, and move an audience have also remained largely unchanged since the time of Ancient Greece. Aristotle, for instance, famously declared that there are three primary means of persuasion—*logos, ethos*, and *pathos*— each of them representing a type of proof employed by the speaker in the oration itself. *Logos* refers to the rational arguments and logical claims made by the speaker to prove the validity of an idea and truth of a statement. For instance, arguments by sign, example, principle, or cause could direct the mind on a path that would make a conclusion seem reasonable and thereby support the aim of *docere*. *Ethos* refers to the credibility and character of the speaker as revealed through the speaker's actions, choice of words, past experiences, and relationship to the audience established through the speech itself. For Aristotle, *ethos* was not something one simply possessed; it was a proof to be constructed in a speech by proving one's virtue, goodwill, and practical wisdom. *Pathos* refers to the passions aroused by the details, narratives, and examples of the speech that provide a type of emotional proof that justified specific attitudes. Aristotle thus carefully defined the emotions and showed how to arouse them through a combination of pleasure and pain in such a way that supported the aim of *movere*. For Aristotle, the true **rhetorician** (that is, a practitioner of rhetoric) was that individual who could step into any situation and find the types of proofs capable of teaching, moving, and delighting an audience in such a way that accomplishes the aims of the speaker.

Finally, the classical tradition has handed down a method of transforming an idea into an effective persuasive performance through the **five canons of rhetoric**, which encompass a system for crafting powerful speeches. These canons form the basis for the early chapters in this book. These canons are invention, arrangement, style, delivery, and memory. *Invention* provides a method of creating effective arguments by focusing our attention on specific resources that might be useful for coming up with good ideas. These resources include public memory, history, books, testimony, and experience. *Arrangement* provides conventional templates or frameworks useful in organizing those things in clear patterns and orders, such as how we organize a speech by topical, causal, or geographical order. *Style* emphasizes the importance of using concrete words, tropes, and figures to communicate complex facts and examples in a way more pleasing and comprehensible images and feelings. *Memory* provides the techniques for committing a speech to memory and making it feel like a natural expression of oneself rather than a written text. Last, *delivery* ensures that the brilliance of the composition is effectively transmitted to the audience through the actions and words of the speaker, including voice, gestures, and eye contact.

To get a sense of how the means and aims of persuasion function in practice, let us look at a traditional example of rhetorical public speaking. On March 7, 2015, President Barack Obama delivered a commemorative speech honoring the 50th anniversary of a watershed moment of the civil rights movement. On March 7, 1965, a group of African-American men and women began marching from Selma, Alabama to Montgomery to protest widespread voting discrimination; they were met with police violence at Edmund Pettus Bridge. The violent scenes of police beating unarmed protesters, including women and children, simply because they wished to acquire the right to vote were shocking to television viewers. At the time, African-Americans made up half of the population of Selma but only 2 percent of registered voters. These protests helped give momentum to the passing of the Voting Rights Act. Obama used this speech to clearly link Selma with the highest American values by drawing on his knowledge of rhetorical techniques:

> As we commemorate their achievement, we are well-served to remember that at the time of the marches, many in power condemned rather than praised them. Back then, they were called Communists, or half-breeds, or outside agitators, sexual and moral degenerates, and worse—they were called everything but the name their parents gave them. Their faith was questioned. Their lives were threatened. Their patriotism challenged. And yet, what could be more American than what happened in this place? What could more profoundly vindicate the idea of America than plain and humble people—unsung, the downtrodden, the dreamers not of high station, not born to wealth or privilege, not of one religious tradition but many, coming together to shape their country's course? What greater expression of faith in the American experiment than this, what greater form of patriotism is there than the belief that America is not yet finished, that we are strong enough to be self-critical, that each successive generation can look upon our imperfections and decide that it is in our power to remake this nation to more closely align with our highest ideals? That's why Selma is not some outlier in the American experience. That's why it's not a museum or a static monument to behold from a distance. It is instead the manifestation of a creed written into our founding documents: "We the People … in order to form a more perfect union."[2]

Obama establishes his **ethos** here through his expression of goodwill toward the citizens who organized for their rights during the Selma march. The rest of the passage is structured as a transition from **pathos** to **logos**. Obama evokes the emotions of courage, indignation, and pride in his narrative account of the suffering, struggle, and overcoming in the first few passages in a way that achieves *movere*. Then he transitions to a principled explanation of

2   Barack Obama, "Remarks by the President at the 50th Anniversary of the Selma to Montgomery Marches," available at www.whitehouse.gov/the-press-office/2015/03/07/remarks-president-50th-anniversary-selma-montgomery-marches (accessed March 24, 2022).

the American character, ending in a quotation from the U.S. Constitution that defines the nation's civic faith in a way that accomplishes *docere*. Within the text, Obama employs figures of **style** like parallelism, alliteration, and rhythm to produce *delectare*. Finally, in composing his oration, he drew from historical resources of **invention** to craft an accurate narrative, **arrangement** to give it structure, **memory** to perform it with a sense of confidence and ease, and **delivery** to add the forcefulness of his voice and expression.

Because these classical categories have demonstrated their enduring value through the centuries, this book will make use of them to organize the chapters and provide a framework for mastering the art of rhetoric. At the same time, this book is not restricted to classical concepts. Rhetorical scholars have continued to refine and develop the equipment for public speaking, and each chapter will make use of these insights and seek innovative ways to adapt the art of rhetoric to the needs of the contemporary student. Rhetoric today is alive as never before, with many of the most powerful voices from young, diverse, and creative members of the new generations for whom communication on video and social media is as natural as speaking in person.

The Rhetorical Situation

One advantage of thinking about public speaking as a rhetorical practice is that it focuses attention on how the art of persuasion functions as a response to a situation. Rather than beginning with the personal interests and desires of the speaker, rhetoric begins with a study of a situation and its relationship to an audience. Rhetoric responds to **contingency**, which is some unexpected obstacle, perplexity, or problem that obstructs our practices or threatens our happiness in some way. Contingencies then become rhetorical concerns when they impact the lives of many people and cause them to deliberate about how best to proceed. Aristotle summed this up best:

> The duty of rhetoric is to deal with such matters as we deliberate upon without arts or systems to guide us … The subjects of our deliberation … present us with alternative possibilities: about things that could not have been, and cannot now or in the future be, other than they are, nobody who takes them to be of this nature wastes his time in deliberation.[3]

We can thus define rhetoric as a type of speech that responds to a **rhetorical situation** that occurs when public contingencies generate concern and uncertainty within a public audience and give force and effectiveness to persuasive discourse that encourages collective action to resolve a problem. In other words, even if a problem exists and a speaker advocates a solution, this

---

3   Aristotle, *Rhetoric*, available at http://classics.mit.edu/Aristotle/rhetoric.1.i.html (accessed March 24, 2022), 1357a.

speech lacks force and effectiveness if an audience does not perceive it as an actual problem.

There are therefore three essential components to a rhetorical situation: exigence, audience, and constraints. An **exigence** is any outstanding aspect of our environment that makes us feel a combination of *concern, uncertainty*, and *urgency*. Not all exigencies are rhetorical. During our everyday lives, we encounter numerous exigencies, both large and small, that require an exertion of energy to deal with and possibly overcome, but these may not call out for any particular rhetorical response. For instance, you may find that your water pipe is broken, and you do not have clean water in your home. But this response simply requires calling a plumber to fix it. No particular rhetorical work is required. However, a specifically *rhetorical* exigence is more than just the existence of a pressing problem; a **rhetorical exigence** must be an issue that generates concern and uncertainty for some group of people that can be resolved, in whole or in part, by persuading an audience to act in a way that is capable of addressing the situation. For instance, in Flint, Michigan, many families discovered that they all were drinking contaminated water due to corroded public water pipes. Finally, **constraints** are anything that limits or restricts action, including objects, resources, laws, habits, time, or knowledge.

Part of the challenge of rhetoric, however, is that often people do not recognize that a problem exists. A **contested exigence** is one in which many people deny the existence of a problem. One goal of rhetoric in this case is to transform it into an **uncontested exigence** that everyone agrees undeniably exists. For instance, for climate scientists, the fact of global warming presents an uncontested exigence for the entire globe. For climate skeptics, global warming remains a dubious theory promoted by alarmists who want to take advantage of people's fears.

The **audience**, therefore, represents any person, or group of people, who hears, reads, or witnesses any communicative event. However, we can break down the concept of audience into three categories: the primary audience, secondary audience, and the target audience. The **primary audience** for rhetorical public speaking consists of those people actually assembled together to hear the speech as it is delivered in person by the speaker. **Secondary audiences** represent all those people who encounter the speech either through some other media or secondhand through the spoken word of another person. But what is most important in rhetoric is the **target audience**, which consists of those individuals or groups in either the primary or secondary audiences who are able to be persuaded and are capable of acting in such a way to help resolve the exigence. Specifying the target audience is essential to helping a speaker develop effective arguments that appeals to the specific needs, concerns, and interests of those who must act in order to effectively resolve the exigence.

Rhetoric is the means by which we encourage audiences to become agents of change to improve their own lives and the lives of others. The fact that most of us seek to make changes on a much smaller scale than social and political leaders does not make our own performances any less rhetorical or less important. Even if we are speaking in front of friends and family on informal occasions, we are still making a difference in people's lives in some way. Thinking of our acts of public speaking rhetorically does not necessitate any particular way of speaking. It simply encourages us to think more deeply about our audience and our shared situation so that we might craft a speech that satisfies their desires.

Speech Genres

Essential to fulfilling the desires of the audience is to recognize that all people approach speeches with the expectations that they will conform to a certain genre. A rhetorical speech **genre** represents a coherent and recognized arrangement of elements in a composition or discourse that is appropriate to certain occasions and that creates audience expectations that constrain and guide a speech's content, style, and delivery. A genre is a method of interpreting a particular type of object, event, or action. Genres are therefore practical tools that speakers can use to anticipate and control the reactions of an audience. Related to notions of appropriateness and occasion, speaking genres refer to what people *actually expect* when they attend a speech, much in the way that rooms in museums are given "generic" labels so that visitors will know what to expect on entering. A speech genre represents a familiar, conventional, and appropriate way of responding to a particular and recognizable type of speech situation. Just as movie genres of horror, action, and romantic comedy help movie-goers know what to expect from a film, speech genres exist in the habits and expectations of a particular culture who have come to expect certain things from a public speech on specific occasions.

Aristotle, who was the first to strictly define speech genres, had the crucial insight that a genre is defined not only by the qualities of the speech itself but also by the expectations of the audience. As he writes: "rhetoric falls into three divisions, determined by the three classes of listeners to speeches. For of the three elements in speechmaking—speaker, subject, and person addressed—it is the last one, the hearer, that determines the speech's end and object."[4] The rhetorical speech genres of deliberative, forensic, and epideictic should therefore be considered *ways of listening* before they should be considered *ways of speaking*.

Any successful speech must begin with a detailed consideration of the expectations of an audience before developing persuasive strategies to meet those expectations. Rather than first asking the question: "What do I want to say?" one should actually begin with the question: "What does my audience want to hear?" For Aristotle, these genres were thus structured by the places in which people came to hear speeches. **Forensic speeches** were

4   Aristotle, *Rhetoric*, 1358b1.

demanded by juries in law courts tasked with deciding the justice or injustice of past actions based on analysis of evidence and inquiry into human motives. **Deliberative speeches** were delivered to citizens in the political assembly who had to compare competing positions that used causal arguments to show how their proposals would be expedient for the future. **Epideictic speeches** were spoken before a gathering of the community at ceremonial events who wished to give glory to the actions of individuals who were held up for praise because they honored the values of that community.

Today, speech genres are even more varied. Certainly, forensic, deliberative, and epideictic speeches still occur in courts, congresses, and commemorations. However, in a complex technological age that communicates through diverse communication platforms, the notion that speech only occurs in three physical contexts is too limited. Our speech genres span multiple contexts and must satisfy general demands that audiences have across situations. Popular textbooks often make the problem worse by using the outdated triad of informative, persuasive, and ceremonial speeches in their designs. No speech is purely informative or persuasive precisely because, as Cicero noted, any speech must teach, move, and delight. Characterizing a speech only as "informative" ignores the pragmatic value of information to resolve a problem, labeling a speech "persuasive" tends to focus on the intention of the speaker rather than the demands of the hearer, while emphasizing the "ceremonial" aspect of speeches reverts to the narrow physical contexts of Aristotle.

Speech genres are defined neither by the intention of the speaker nor the physical context of the speech but by the manner in which the speech satisfies the different motives of an audience. Specifically, genres develop in relation to the **interests, beliefs**, and **values** of an audience. A **belief** is a statement of fact on which a person is prepared to act. Our beliefs form the set of core statements that we trust represent factual reality, such as "everyone loves their children" or "free trade produces prosperity" or "college is important for career advancement." A **value** is an abstract ideal quality that guides our behavior across a variety of situations and tells us what is worthwhile and worth preserving. For instance, "love is more important than gold" or "freedom is the essence of human life" or "educating the mind is an end in itself." An **interest** is a set of practical actions or objective things that an audience sees as directly improving their well-being. Whereas values are abstract and general, interests are concrete and specific. For instance, "the modern family needs affordable housing" or "a nation's economic well-being depends on trade agreements" or "a person needs a college degree to work in Silicon Valley."

Contemporary speech genres must begin by identifying the needs of the audience to whom one is addressing within circumstances that are often more informal and multifaceted. For instance, the economic incentive to sell products or fund-raise makes **solicitation** speeches an ever-present fact of life, in which we are asked to invest money in the name of mutual interests. The fact that our complex social life demands joining a multiplicity of groups, often simultaneously, makes **introduction** speeches essential to forming social relationships. The need to constantly reaffirm enthusiastic group identity demands speeches of **encouragement** whose focus is the re-performance of established group values. Taking on leadership roles within those groups then demands mastery of **administrative** speeches to justify policy decisions and improve the procedures and communication structures of an organization. And especially with the rise of social media, departures from groups have given rise to a new genre of **invective** speeches designed to attack the presumptions and expose the hypocrisies of those same groups to which one belonged. Any casual scrolling through our social media accounts will undoubtedly show any number of these speech genres occurring simultaneously.

For the purposes of instruction, however, this book will focus only on what are arguably the three major speech genres: enrichment, advocacy, and commemoration. An **enrichment** speech satisfies the preexisting interests of an audience by showing them how to attain their desires and overcome obstacles more effectively. An enrichment speech does not ask an audience to alter its views or beliefs. It simply takes their interests as they are and gives them better instruction, based on a combination of experience and knowledge, on how to achieve them. Speeches of enrichment are generally given in situations in which an audience has already acknowledged its lack of awareness about some problem or issue and has voluntarily attended an occasion to gain this knowledge in order to resolve a situation (such as learning how to get a job in a bad economy), to satisfy curiosity (such as learning about the latest discoveries of planets outside our solar system), or to enrich one's life (such as learning how to appreciate good wine). The speaker will present information in an entertaining but *noncontroversial* manner such that he or she is not advocating a particular position. For once audience members feel that they are not being informed, but being manipulated or pushed, they will no longer receive the information as a gift for enrichment, but as an active solicitation.

An **advocacy** speech satisfies an audience's desire for growth by showing how certain beliefs should be adopted over others because they are both truer and ethically superior. Unlike an enrichment speech, advocacy speeches directly challenge the beliefs of an audience and seek to change them. However, this act of persuasion is done in order to help them achieve some larger life goal. The term "advocacy" is used in the sense that the speaker is an "advocate," which is literally defined as one who speaks on behalf of something or someone else, as when we might "advocate" for a friend by using our influence with others to help that friend. This means that speeches of advocacy always speak "on behalf" of some higher cause or ideal that transcends the self-interest of the speaker or even of the audience. It is in this way that an advocate might criticize members of an audience for being too concerned with their own immediate problems and not willing to sacrifice time and effort to strive for something greater than their own self-advancement. It therefore "advocates for" an idea by showing how it should hold a greater place in people's lives and thoughts than it currently does. For instance, one might advocate for greater sacrifice to save the environment, for overcoming biases against some social group, or for severely limiting social media usage to spend more time with family.

Lastly, a **commemorative** speech satisfies an audience's need to establish common bonds with one another by celebrating specific values through honoring those people and events that reflect the higher ideals of a community. Like epideictic and ceremonial speeches, commemorative speeches generate solidarity among a community. A commemorative speech brings people together to honor the values that unite them as a group and that are embodied in their members and their actions. Consequently, any group or institution that relies on the motivation of its members makes frequent use of commemorative speeches both to inspire excellence and to create a shared sense of commitment. Even commemorating loved ones at a funeral binds people together in a uniquely powerful way by using their stories to create a sense of reverence and legacy. Thus, although speeches of commemoration often do not usually argue specific points, they create and reinforce the values on which people often rely when called to make concrete judgments in practice. In speaking to the past and future, they endeavor to create a lasting impression in historical time. Commemorative speeches might honor the influence of a teacher who instilled the value of learning, the love of a parent who taught the value of hard work, or the courage of a soldier who died defending the values of liberty.

Monroe's Motivated Sequence

To bring all these elements together, a good place to start is **Monroe's motivated sequence**. Alan Monroe was a professor of speech at Purdue University who developed a special sequence designed for policy speeches that encourage immediate action. What he wanted to create was a method of arousing an audience's desires and then moving them, through the use of visual narrative, toward a promised satisfaction that results in concrete judgment and action. In effect, what he provided was a compressed and streamlined form of arrangement adaptable to solicitation, deliberation, and advocacy speeches. Monroe's motivated sequence therefore provides a helpful starting place to experience how the art of rhetoric can help produce innovative and engaging speeches. Not surprisingly, one can find this sequence imitated frequently in advertisements, in particular those for pharmaceutical products, which use this model almost exclusively. The five steps of attention, need, satisfaction, visualization, and action each draw from different rhetorical categories as follows:

1   *Attention* ("what's new?"). The Attention getter is a striking and concrete story, fact, quote, engaging question, statistic, or image that grabs the attention of the audience and makes them want to listen to you as the speaker. The purpose of Attention is to "wake up" an audience by cutting through the noise and clutter of everyday communication and confronting them with something unusual, interesting, startling, curious, dangerous, or enticing. Typically, Attention relies on using some form of **pathos** to move the emotions of an audience (*movere*) and emphasizes the need for a confident, passionate, and spontaneous **delivery**. For instance: "*Did you know that, right now, that there is 100,000 tons of garbage floating in a patch of the Pacific Ocean three times the size of Texas? Well there is. And it is appropriately called the Great Pacific Garbage Patch.*"

2   *Need* ("what's wrong?"). Need establishes the necessity to address some issue by graphically and clearly defining a problem that confronts the audience in the present. Need does not tell us how to solve this problem; that is the function of Satisfaction. It simply defines the problem itself and relates it directly to the lives of the people listening. Need draws both **logos**, to define the nature and causes of the problem (*docere*), as well as **pathos**, to continue evoking emotions that are connected in some form with pain, whether present or future, that we desire to eliminate (*movere*). For instance: "*This enormous pile of garbage is not simply ugly, but dangerous. Large pieces of plastic can trap animals or accumulate in their stomachs. And plastic also breaks into microplastics which block sunlight, kill algae, and disrupt the marine ecosystem, including productive fisheries. Lastly, they leach harmful pollutants which directly harm humans.*"

3   *Satisfaction* ("how do I fix it?"). Once the Need is defined, Satisfaction lays out what is required to be done for audience members to confront the problem effectively and bring it to resolution. In Satisfaction, a speaker should provide step-by-step instructions as to how to solve the problem, addressing issues like what resources are required, cost, accessibility, time, when this needs to happen, who will be involved, and what method must be employed. Because of its logical nature, Satisfaction tends to rely on a combination of **logos**, to provide careful logical instruction (*docere*), and **ethos**, which provides the credibility necessary to convince an audience of one's expertise. For instance: "*Fortunately, one project is under way to remedy the problem. It is funded by the non-profit Ocean Cleanup, which has the goal of removing 90 percent of floating ocean plastic by 2040. Guided by two boats, their half-mile-long installation catches large and small debris from the seawater in a funnel-shaped net. Because it remains small scale, it has only made a slight impact. But with funding, more can be achieved.*"

4   *Visualization* ("what would success look like?"). The step of Visualization is where the speaker moves beyond **logos** and gives full reign to **style** which both delights the ear (*delectare*) as well as uses **pathos** to paint an image of a better future that replaces anxiety of pain with desire for

pleasure (*movere*). This step relies on heightening emotions by visualizing the wonderful state of affairs that will occur after satisfaction. Visualization thus projects an audience into the future and asks them to "imagine" how their lives might look after a successful Satisfaction. For instance: "*Imagine an ocean no longer choked with plastic bottles, old fishing line, broken toys, shopping bags, and medicine bottles. Instead, one would see the rolling waves reflecting the bright sun with only the shadows of birds drifting across its surface.*"

5   *Action* ("what can I do now?"). Now that the audience has been suitably inspired, this step tells them what they can do to get started by performing some specific task right away. Action does not repeat Satisfaction. It focuses on getting an audience to take the first step by pointing to some simple, easy, and immediate task. The purpose is to break an audience out of their inertia and get them moving toward a goal. This step relies heavily on **ethos** to convince them to act based both on a speaker's character and their own collective identity. For instance: "*We all are part of this natural world. We live in it as we live in our own homes. I have walked beaches in the Pacific that were literally covered in garbage that simply washed ashore, spending days helping restore the sands. Let us clean up our home and support the funding to make Ocean Cleanup a reality.*"

Because of the simplicity and clarity of its steps, Monroe's motivated sequence is an ideal starting point to understand the importance of form to rhetorical persuasion. It is a method that applies not only to advertising but also to politics and social action. Once you become familiar with the patterns of persuasion embodied in this structure, you can begin developing your own style that fits your needs and satisfies your audience.

Practical Judgment

As demonstrated by Monroe's motivated sequence, the goal of rhetorical public speaking is to advocate for some practical judgment on the part of the audience. A **practical judgment** is an act of categorizing a particular person, object, or event in a way that encourages a specific attitude and culminates in some future action. In other words, practical judgments tell us *what subjects concern us, what they are,* and *what we should do in response to them.* The mere giving of commands—such as "Go!" or "Halt!"—is therefore *not* a practical judgment because it does not satisfy the first criterion of the definition. A practical judgment encourages action, but such an action is the outcome of a reasoned conclusion, not a mere command. The best way to think of practical judgments is through the analogy of a court trial. The jury must consider the arguments of the prosecution and defense before arriving at a verdict which decides guilt or innocence. Whether a defendant is set free or goes to prison is a practical judgment.

Practical judgments thus result from a connection between a *subject*, an *idea*, and an *action*. For instance, "the weather outside (*subject*) is freezing (*idea*), so make sure you wear a jacket (*action*)." Or, "this segregation law (*subject*) is unjust (*idea*) and must be found unconstitutional (*action*)." Or, "too much exposure to social media (*subject*) can be addicting (*idea*) and should therefore be restricted in young children (*action*)." Rhetoric involves the struggle to properly name and categorize things so that one type of practical judgment seems more reasonable and effective than another. The question of practical judgment thus centers around the matter of naming and therefore of meaning. We must be very careful with the words we use to describe our environment, because every word is loaded with particular denotations and connotations and associations that inevitably lead people to act in certain ways.

Discussion Questions

1   In what situations in your lives are you most influenced by face-to-face communication?
2   For what everyday problems do you actively seek out digital social influencers?
3   For each of these above situations, identify its type of speech genre.
4   What types of rhetorical situations are featured in today's news and social media? Break does each of its aspects.
5   Identify a popular commercial that you have seen. How does it achieve the three aims of Cicero, to move, to delight, and to teach?
6   When have you engaged in rhetoric with your friends and family? Give specific examples and identify the qualities of the rhetorical situation (exigence, audience, and constraints) to which you responded.
7   Find a video advertisement that follows Monroe's motivated sequence and break down each of its steps.
8   Name a practical judgment, no matter how trivial, that you have made in the past day that resulted from a process of deliberation. How would you phrase it in a sentence?

Exercises

1   **Monroe's motivated sequence**: Write a speech using Monroe's motivated sequence. Each speaker should develop a unique and fantastic product (no matter how unrealistic) that would satisfy the needs of the audience. Convince the audience to buy the product.
2   **Practical judgment**: Write a one-sentence practical judgment about an ordinary object that forces an audience to adopt a new perspective on its value, whether it be making it worse or better. In that speech, make sure to appeal explicitly to ethos, pathos, and logos in three different arguments that defend this judgment.
3   **Rhetorical situation**: Define a rhetorical situation that you believe affects ordinary students every day. Work to transform a contested

exigence into an uncontested one. Define the exigence, audience, and constraints in your speech, and be sure to explain what actions the audience can take collectively to remedy the situation.

References

Aristotle, *Rhetoric*, available at http://classics.mit.edu/Aristotle/rhetoric.1.i.html (accessed March 24, 2022).

Obama, Barack. "Remarks by the President at the 50th Anniversary of the Selma to Montgomery Marches," available at www.whitehouse.gov/the-press-office/2015/03/07/remarks-president-50th-anniversary-selma-montgomery-marches (accessed March 24, 2022).

Ong, Walter. *Orality and Literacy: The Technologizing of the Word* (New York: Routledge, 2002).

2 Digital Social Influencing

Much of what we used to communicate in face-to-face settings is now done online, particularly through video posts on social media. Although traditional rhetorical techniques remain effective, we must also attend to the changes that modern digital technology has introduced. Digital communication refers to text, image, audio, and video messages sent and received by individuals on computer-aided technologies and capable of being received simultaneously by an infinite number of users and also being recalled by those users at any time. One of the genres introduced by this technology is **digital social influencing** that generates a large online audience of enthusiastic, engaged followers who pay close attention to the regular posts of those content generators who they find credible, entertaining, and like-minded. Digital social influencing therefore refers to a type of public speaking in which individuals speak directly to the audience but do so not from a conventional public speaking context, like an auditorium, rostrum, or shared space, but from more intimate or on-site locations that imitate television journalistic techniques. It is not simply a long public speech recorded and rebroadcast online. Social influencing is designed specifically for the video medium and makes use of film-style editing, broadcast news style graphics and voiceovers, and a more direct and "close-up" style of delivery. Generally, this type of digital rhetoric is highly condensed and short enough to be viewed within a couple of minutes or even a few seconds. Many of the most viewed social influencer posts are no more than thirty seconds long.

There are several specific features of online digital communication that make it distinct from face-to-face oral performance. First, it allows for multiple messages to be sent and received simultaneously and at rapid speed. This creates an enormous competition for a viewer's attention, as it creates an almost permanent backlog of messages awaiting consideration. In this environment, messages are naturally crafted to capture one's immediate attention and be received and understood in a short amount of time. Second, the capability of multimedia messaging further heightens this sense of competition. A simple email or text, for instance, might be supplemented with embedded images, attached files, and background graphics or sound.

DOI: 10.4324/9781003316787-2

Third, it creates a situation of receiving a message in private while it is capable of being broadcast to a group. This reduces the sense of "privacy" that oral speech tends to produce while at the same time allowing a message to be freed from its situational context. Fourth, the capability of saving and resending messages allows them to spread widely and rapidly, thereby allowing both successes and mistakes to be immediately broadcast to all members of a group, from a group of friends to a global audience. Fifth, the storage capabilities of online digital communication make a message endure potentially forever, as long as it is retrievable. Digital communication has the paradoxical quality of being both ephemeral and eternal.

Today, **digital social influencing** has become something of a profession. A **social influencer** is a content creator who has attracted a large social media following and who uses their perceived credibility, expertise, and likeability to persuade this following to adopt practices, buy products, or favor certain services. Social influencers come from all walks of life. Sometimes they are insiders who have established a significant amount of online credibility in their field or industry. Other times they are well-known celebrities or athletes who transfer their popularity from one sphere to another. And very often they are ordinary people who have attracted an audience due to their charisma and creativity. The vast majority are young. But all social influencers thrive because their audience feels that their advice and endorsements are particularly authentic and trustworthy.

In rhetorical terms, social influencers rely almost exclusively on creating an **ethos** that attracts and engages an audience to the degree that it becomes committed to their message. And this ethos is profitable. Financially, social influencers profit from a combination of sources. First, on digital platforms that feature advertising, social influencers who have garnered enough reliable followers can "sell" that audience to advertisers for a profit. Second, social influencers can be paid directly by producers of goods and services to promote their products to their followers. Third, successful social influencers, such as fitness instructors or other trainers, can sell direct subscriptions. Lastly, social influencers can often work with affiliates to design and sell their own products. However, regardless of the process of monetization, all of these strategies require as a baseline the ability to produce video content that captures the attention and interest of an audience. No business model is worth anything without effective content creation that relies on mastery of the skills in public speaking adapted for the video medium.

This chapter will examine the profession of social influencing and explore the basic techniques of composing, recording, and editing a speech to be disseminated on a digital platform. Of course, one need not aspire to be a professional social influencer to make use of these techniques. Learning how to adapt the rhetorical techniques of public speaking to communication through digital platforms is a valuable skill in many spheres of life. Many universities require video submissions on applications, businesses often recommend creating a digital presence to generate brand loyalty, teachers and coaches can use them to instruct their students and players, and of course everyday social media users can make use of them in their communication with friends and family. However, this chapter focuses on social influencing because it synthesizes the most effective techniques into one practice.

How to Not Influence Anyone

With just a few basic pieces of equipment set up in a carefully planned space, you can already begin to approximate a more professional look to your videos. Anyone can record themselves talking in front of a computer webcam and post it unedited online; but almost no one would want to watch such a thing. Today, with the almost infinite number of videos vying for our attention, even the most powerful speech delivered with the best arguments will go unseen if it lacks production value. To get started, there are a few basic rules to follow in terms of what *not* to do when recording your speech. First, these are the things you should avoid:

1 *Don't make it all about you.* Social influence is not about you. It is about your audience. When you are creating content, think first of how whatever you say satisfies the beliefs, values, and interests of your audience. Never assume that anyone will watch your video simply because it is there. Neither you nor your subject matter has intrinsic value. You have to constantly work to relate yourself and your subject to the viewers who are taking the time to listen.
2 *Do not use built-in laptop webcams.* Laptop computers have notoriously grainy video images and poor sound quality. Only use these as a last resort. They make watching the recording uncomfortable on the eye and the ear.
3 *Do not record using the wrong orientation.* If you are using a smartphone video camera to record a video to be seen on a computer, do not record yourself holding the phone vertically (that is, like the "portrait" orientation). Not only does this restrict your gestures and show too much space above and below your face, but also when viewed on a computer it will show two black bars to the left and right. Alternately, do not record horizontally (that is, like the "landscape" orientation) if you are recording a video to be viewed exclusively on a smartphone, or the reverse will happen, and you will have huge black bars at the top and bottom.
4 *Do not allow backlighting.* Backlighting is when you have a direct source of light directly behind you when being recorded. These sources might include an open window behind your head, a lamp on a nearby desk, or a mirror on the wall. Not only is a bright light source districting, but backlighting forces the camera to compensate for the brightness by reducing the overall exposure, which has the effect of putting one's face into shadow. Never have any direct light source shining on the camera.

5   *Do not use ambient microphones.* An ambient microphone is one designed to pick up diffuse room sounds. These are microphones that are often used for group meetings that one can place at the center of a table. A smartphone or a laptop webcam effectively acts like an ambient microphone when one's voice is a few feet away. Ambient microphones give the voice an echo-like quality and often include too much background noise and hisses.

6   *Do not record yourself against a wall.* Often, beginner speakers record themselves with the wall directly behind them, sometimes sitting in a chair. A blank wall is not only unappealing but gives the impression of being in a police line-up. One's voice echoes off of the wall and the lights create dark shadows behind one's head. This also goes for bookcases, curtains, or any other flat background.

7   *Do not record the ceiling.* Especially when people record themselves on laptops which are below eye-level, there is a tendency to speak "down" to the computer. With the camera tilted up, the screen becomes filled with dark corners of rooms, ceiling fans, and backlighting, not to mention the inside of one's nose. At no point should the ceiling of your room appear in your video except in the distance.

8   *Do not get lost in your space.* When the camera is too far away or lacks proper zoom, the person who is speaking can get lost in the clutter of a space. Especially when the filming location is a dormitory room or kitchen that may have odd or unique elements, all of the items in the room can distract attention away from the speaker.

9   *Do not overuse voiceover.* People watch social influencing videos in order to see the person speaking. A social influencer gains followers because they provide what sociologists call "parasocial interaction," which is a feeling that people are having a genuine relationship with someone in the media that they do not actually know. Voiceovers not only lack intimacy, but they are ineffective modes of delivery.

10   *Do not fill the screen with still photos or imported video clips.* Content creators must create their own content. Just as you should avoid too much voiceover, you should also not create a "slideshow" that hides behind other media.

In summary, poor videos are those in which the speaker tries to recreate a "natural" public speaking environment that is largely unconcerned with the practicalities of video production. In other words, speakers set up an ambient microphone and camera in one corner of a room and then stand somewhere on the screen and deliver a speech as they would if they were speaking to someone in the room with them. This is the completely wrong way to think about digital social influencing. Although you desire to address an audience of actual human beings, you have to imagine yourself speaking first to the camera and the microphone.

Three-Point Photography Set-Up

Creating a workable production space requires minimal investment in technology, but these investments are necessary to be successful in digital social influencing. The ideal is an intimate, well-lighted space that reflects your personality, reduces outside noise to a minimum, and makes you feel comfortable. If you were to imagine the camera as a live audience, it should be as if it were a close friend sitting across from you, having a personal conversation. Below are some of the essential tools you require and how they should be used.

1 *A smartphone.* The cameras on most smartphones today are excellent. If you already own one, this is the simplest way to capture clear and vivid video. Acceptable replacements might also be a good external webcam that plugs into a computer using a USB port or a professional digital camera capable of recording video. However, learning to use a smartphone to record video is often preferable because of its portability. The instructions that follow will assume smartphone usage.

2 *A selfie-stick tripod.* You will need a portable tripod capable of gripping a smartphone and positioning it at eye-level. Often, these tripods also come with a small Bluetooth remote control that allows you to turn the video camera on and off from a distance.

3 *An LED ring light.* These lights are 8–12 inches in diameter and are typically placed directly above and behind the camera in order to provide "front lighting" on one's face. They should come with adjustable colors and brightness levels. This light should also come with a tripod of its own.

4 *A lavalier microphone.* For good sound quality, a lavalier microphone that can clip onto your shirt is an absolute essential. Inexpensive ones can be purchased that have a long cord to plug into a phone that you can thread underneath your shirt. Preferable are those connected using a Bluetooth adapter and allow for more freedom of movement (although make sure this adapter can be plugged into a phone's headphone jack and does not use a USB connection for a computer). A lesser alternative is using the earphones/ear pods that came with your phone, although the recording quality is inferior to a lavalier microphone.

5 *Free video editing software.* You will need access to basic video editing software that can cut and combine multiple video files, add captions, overlay photographs, and create smooth transitions. There are many free apps to choose from that can serve these needs. You do not need expensive, high-end editing software for digital social influencing. Find the simplest application with accompanying video tutorials to use for your videos.

6 *Fill lights.* The ring light on its own is insufficient for creating a comfortable look. To accomplish this atmosphere, you also need lights to the side and above and behind you (but NOT directly in the camera

frame—see the warning about backlighting). For amateur productions, simple desk and floor lamps with shades should be sufficient. You can also simply purchase a set of ring lights on tripods.

7   *A comfortable space.* You need little more than an 8-foot-square space to effectively construct a setting for filming. The space should feel intimate and conversational. You should neither have your back against a wall nor have behind you a large, empty space. Also, you should not film yourself in front of a window, even when the shades are drawn. The background should be about 5 feet behind you and be uncluttered but still reflect your personality. In a dormitory, for instance, you might film yourself sitting on your bed or seated at your desk. Having plants, photos, colorful holiday lights, stuffed animals, sports equipment, mugs, flowers, musical instruments, posters, tapestries, books, and other personal decor in the background can contribute a lot to establishing *ethos*.

With all of this equipment, you should try to approximate what is called the "three-point lighting" set-up for photography. First, find a location in the middle of your room where you can sit or stand comfortably. Make sure you look relaxed and have freedom of movement. Second, make sure you have no distracting sources of backlighting, especially windows. Third, set up your camera tripod a few feet away and at eye level. Do not position it below you. Fourth, position the "key light" (the LED ring light) so that it shines directly on your face, but slightly at an angle to one side on the camera. Do not put it right behind the camera or your pupils will reflect the ring light. Fifth, set up a "fill light" (for instance, a desk lamp) on the other side of the camera so that it brightens the other side of your face. Your camera should now be between two sources of front lighting. Sixth, set up a "backlight" behind and to one side of you so that it does not appear directly in the camera frame. You want to avoid creating negative "backlighting." Instead, place the lamp to provide ambient "backlight" to get rid of shadows. This can either be a floor lamp or even just the regular ceiling lights if they are placed correctly. Seventh, set up your environment so that it reflects your character and creates an attractive environment. Avoid bare walls and empty shelves. Lastly, plug your lavalier microphone into your phone. You are now ready to record!

Techniques for Video Recording and Editing

The way we view a video of a speech is very different than how we experience a speech in person. As explained in the first chapter, face-to-face public speaking is a whole-body experience in which the speech is just one part of a whole. Although we might be listening to someone speak, we may be simultaneously eating and drinking, sitting in a shared space, listening to side-conversations, or looking out the window. But what is most important is that we cannot simply leave at any time without physically exiting the space. Consequently, a large part of effective rhetorical public speaking is creating a physical atmosphere in which people feel comfortable. As seen in live awards shows, for instance, this can require significant investment.

What makes digital social influencing so ubiquitous is also makes it ephemeral. Because we encounter these speeches on a digital medium, they can be viewed in any circumstance whatsoever. They can be viewed in their entirety or in fragments. They can be watched all at once or at different times. They are often viewed on smartphones when people are busy doing other activities, such as walking across campus, riding a bus, having a coffee, or using the bathroom. And when we view these videos, we always have other things we might be viewing. With the proliferation of social media platforms, we live in a saturated environment of possible videos clamoring for our attention. Any video designed for digital social influence must therefore be created with the awareness that it must outcompete competitors. Simply recording a standard face-to-face speech and posting it online is not sufficient. You must think of a video-recorded speech as a distinct artifact with its own distinct character.

The following techniques are essential to producing engaging, personal videos:

1 *Use close-ups.* Generally speaking, you want the camera frame to include your face and upper torso, providing you enough room to use hand gestures comfortably. Avoid too much empty space above your head. If you are sitting cross-legged on a couch or bed, you can include your whole body. But if you are standing or sitting, film yourself from the waist-up. As a rule, your body should take up no less than a third of the screen. If you are using a smartphone, you might have to use the zoom function on the phone. Avoid getting too close to the camera in a way that distorts your features with a wide-angle lens.

2 *Record the speech in short sections.* Unlike rhetorical public speaking, digital social influencing does not require a single continuous performance. Take advantage of the opportunity to rehearse short sections of the speech one at a time, usually between 10 and 20 seconds in length. When you record, make sure you provide a second of quiet space before and after each recording to allow for room to make transitions.

3 *Memorize each section one at a time.* The visible presence of notecards is not acceptable in digital social influencing. Each performance should feel conversational and spontaneous. Nor is reading a transcript from a computer off-screen an effective method, because the camera will pick up the movement of your eyes and you will lose the personal touch. At the most, one should post key ideas, in the form of notecords, above the camera. But you should always speak as if it was an impromptu performance.

4 *Speak at a brisk, conversational rate.* Digital public speaking often has a faster rate than rhetorical public speaking. Because a video has far less information to process than a live situation, viewers can process words quicker and have less patience. Viewers prefer an informal, personal delivery that

imitates how they might speak to a friend. Avoid the formalities of public address and use a more light-hearted, informal style.

5   *Use hand gestures.* In imitation of everyday conversation, use gestures and facial expressions to create a feeling of engagement. Avoid simply being a talking head. Allow your body to use the space in a way that signals how comfortable you are in the space. Similarly, experiment with exaggerated facial expressions to exploit the close-up filming.

6   *Alter the camera angle a few times between scenes.* Viewers like variety in perspective. Experiment with slightly shifting the camera angle at specific points in the speech. Sometimes you can angle the camera so that it looks like you are speaking to a person just slightly to the left of the camera. Or sometimes you can literally turn toward a new camera angle as if you were speaking to another person. Often this strategy is used to give the impression of speaking an "aside," which is a technique used in theater when a character addresses the audience directly in a way that the other characters cannot hear. This can be used effectively when done with a sense of humor.

7   *Go "on location" to fit the topic.* Although most of your speech will probably be recorded in your organized space, adding scenes filmed "on location" in outdoor spaces can be very effective. Try to find a day when the sun is not too direct. A mild, overcast day without wind is ideal. The filming techniques should be otherwise the same.

8   *Use quick cut transitions.* Because of the quick pace of video creative content, you should avoid the use of transitions between scenes such as fade-to-black or swipe. Try to simply move directly from one scene to another, cutting out any dead spaces. Similarly, if during filming there are periods of long silences, simply cut out those scenes using the "razor" tool in your editing software.

9   *Use subtle captions.* One thing digital social influencing does better than rhetorical public speaking is the subtle but effective use of captions to highlight ideas, quotes, statistics, or the main idea of the speech. Do not overuse captions. However, they can be very effective in signposting the main ideas. Have the captions appear in small but visible text along the bottom of the screen.

10   *Use embedded images.* Another benefit of the editing software is to be able to embed images onto the screen in a way that is subtle. Like a news broadcast, social influencers can make smaller images appear in the upper corners of the video while they are speaking, thus providing examples of what they are discussing while keeping themselves on the screen. Especially effective is when the speaker can "gesture" toward the image as if it were literally hovering over their shoulder before disappearing again.

11   *Keep it short.* Effective social influencer content must conform to the demands for brevity. That means keeping a speech between 1 and 5 minutes long. Around 3 minutes, or the length of a typical popular

song, is something of an ideal. Any longer than that will significantly decrease its influence. However, because of the filming and editing techniques, the content of a video can equal or even surpass the amount of information communicated during a face-to-face public speech twice the length.

The videos produced for digital social influencing, however, are not just information delivery mechanisms. People only seek out this information to the extent that they find the content creator trustworthy, charismatic, and engaging. Maintaining this *ethos* should be foremost on your mind whenever you are speaking. Never assume that the importance of the message justifies a bland or formal delivery. No matter the subject matter, treat the camera as if it was an intimate friend with whom you are having a lively conversation.

How to Become a Social Influencer

Although most of the readers of this chapter may not become social influencers, exploring the nature of the profession illuminates important qualities of **digital rhetoric**, which is any form of public speaking designed to be disseminated in video form online. Through decades of experience, social influencers have developed basic rules to the art of digital rhetoric. The way digital platforms are designed have helped facilitate this process of trial and error. Unlike rhetorical public speaking, where the feedback may be immediate and tactile but yet hard to quantify, digital platforms provide clear metrics to measure success in terms of subscriptions, followers, retweets, likes, and comments. Of course, the proliferation of "bots," or fake accounts that are basically computer algorithms, have complicated these statistics. Judging popularity now requires not only "doing the math" but distinguishing a live follower from a bot. However, those digital social influencers who have risen to the top of popularity and have attracted actual human followers have reaffirmed a few basic principles that are useful for any content creator.

1   *Find a niche.* A **niche** is a position or activity that suits your talents and personality. As the word implies, a niche is a small but distinct place within a larger environment. You "carve out" a niche by placing all of your focus on that one activity or interest without straying outside of it. A niche differentiates you from all of the other millions of people on social media. To find your niche, consider your future goals, your present interests, your target audience, your unique experience, and your expertise. A niche can be anything from ice fishing to financial investment, from dieting to drag racing, from travel to tennis. A successful niche will be focused enough to be unique and yet complex enough to justify different topics and perspectives.

2   *Identify a target audience.* Like any effective rhetoric, successful social influencing requires a speaker to identify one's **target audience** very clearly, which in social influencing represents the specific group of people you want to reach with your message, your brand, and your products. Although one's actual audience is almost always more diverse than this group, the target audience represents the character of your core followers who will determine your success or failure. A target audience should be defined through empirical data, including such categories as age, wealth, hobbies, geography, gender, profession, ethnicity, education, language, and nationality. Once this target audience is identified, limit your message to what satisfies their interests.

3   *Tell a good story.* Part of establishing your niche is being able to tell your **story**, which is a narrative of where you came from, where you are, and where you are going. A story gives you character, goals, a past, expertise, and personality. People like to follow individuals with whom they identify, respect, and like. Being a social influencer requires more than just disseminating useful information. It involves constantly telling and retelling relevant and interesting stories about your life experience that dramatizes and personalizes your message.

4   *Have a powerful message.* What makes your story appealing to an audience is that it gives credibility and power to your **message**, which represents the values, interests, and goals you are trying to communicate to others to enrich their lives. A powerful message is more than just a series of helpful tips. A powerful message challenges and inspires an audience and encourages them to have higher aims and ambitions. Also, a powerful message is personal and direct. Digital social influencers speak forcefully and directly to the camera in order to reach out and motivate their followers.

5   *Produce valuable and free creative content.* In the terminology of social influencing, **creative content** refers to the accessible and appealing media that promotes specific practices, products, and services by building trust and rapport with customers. Unlike traditional advertising, which aggressively seeks to break into the consciousness of its audience through direct marketing, creative content relies on attracting an audience because of its own intrinsic appeal. Consequently, creative content must always aim to meet some need, gratify some interest, or satisfy some curiosity of its target audience. Even though social influencers often profit by marketing certain merchandise, they should never appear as if they are simply salespeople. The choice to promote specific products and services should always be presented as if the social influencer has selected from a variety of options and has selected the best means to satisfy an audience's desires.

6   *Be consistent and authentic.* The gold standard of digital social influencing is **authenticity**, which is the quality of being perceived as real, true,

and genuine. Authenticity is not something communicated in a single message. It develops over time by having been honest, trustworthy, spontaneous, and concerned with the well-being of others ahead of the speaker's self-interest and profit. The moment an audience feels they are being manipulated or treated simply as just another consumer; a social influencer will lose authenticity. Consequently, even when social influencers promote certain products or services, they must show how their choice grew out of their own personal experience and commitments combined with a thoughtful analysis of the audience's needs. As a result, social influencers must be consistent in their principles. If a speaker shifts their commitments, they show they are unreliable and are only interested in short-term gain.

7   *Build a sense of community through continuous engagement.* On social media, a **community** represents a group of people who are connected on a network because they wish to communicate about shared interests. Social influencers thrive because they show themselves to be an active part of a community. This means engaging with a community through many social media platforms, posting messages using common hashtags, and commenting on and sharing the posts of others. If a social influencer only posts videos that promote their brands and ideas, then they appear as just another traditional salesperson. Effective social influencing requires continuous engagement, even if it is simply posting comments or "liking" the posts of others. At best, a social influencer should become a hub for that community itself, bringing people together because they all are attracted to the niche you have carved for yourself and wish to share with them.

Conclusion

Even if you do not aspire to be a social influencer, the techniques that have proven successful for them are universally applicable. Their experience clearly shows that people consume digital rhetoric because they see it as satisfying their interests, providing a connection with community, establishing a relationship with the speaker, and gratifying some pleasure or curiosity. What is important to keep in mind is that these expectations do not change because the context, speaker, or message changes. As Cicero argued, all audiences wish to be moved, delighted, and instructed. No matter the subject matter of the speech, videos that are posted to be consumed on social media must compete with other creative content. Regardless of what you believe to be the importance of your message, significance alone does not attract an audience. Effective digital social influencing requires a speaker to begin with the needs of an audience and craft a message that communicates credibility, intimacy, and authenticity.

Discussion Questions

1   When have you been without access to online forms of communication for an extended length of time? What did you feel you were missing?
2   Think of when you got your first smartphone as a child. How did it alter your communication and relationships with others?
3   Is face-to-face communication more "genuine" and "honest" than digital forms of communication? For instance, it is a cultural maxim that genuine sincerity and trust can only be insured when you "look a person in the eye." Do you think this is true?
4   Do you follow any social influencers? What do they do for you? And what genres of speech do they tend to use?
5   What constitutes "authenticity" on digital platforms? Do you think authenticity exists or it is all just a performance?
6   Are there any subjects or messages that simply cannot be communicated well through digital social influencing compared to other media?
7   Do you aspire to make money from being a digital social influencer? Or even if not, what are the attractions of this type of work?
8   Does digital social influencing make the world a better place?

Exercises

1   **Introduce your environment**: Record a short introductory speech in which you simply talk about some of the interesting things in your dormitory, apartment, or room. Practice using quick editing so that you are able to cut together multiple scenes showcasing different objects without any transitions or gaps. The video should be short but packed with different images and objects in order to get a sense of what is interesting about your surroundings, and which demonstrates something about yourself.
2   **Identify your brand**: Create a social influencing "persona" that you might use to attract an audience. Record an introduction speech in which you give yourself a catchy name and tries to carve a niche for yourself based on something you are actually interested in. Make sure in your video that you show some objects that connect in some way to your brand and the interests of your target audience.
3   **Perform a demonstration**: Make a video that works through, step by step, some action that you know how to do that might interest your audience. Explain why this action is important and describe how to do it well. In your video, make sure to use captions, multiple perspectives, and at least one change of scene.

3 Memory and Delivery

The canons of delivery and memory are closely related. **Memory** refers to the firm retention in the mind of the matter, words, and arrangement of a speech that can be quickly recalled during delivery. Committing a speech to memory makes the words feel more natural, comfortable, and spontaneous, allowing the speaker to focus more on the audience. Good memory then facilitates effective **delivery,** which deals with the manner in which a speaker physically performs the speech through the crafted use of the voice and gesture. Delivery is what makes a speech feel like a personal expression of the speaker, communicating a richer variety of emotions and relationships through both verbal and nonverbal communication. Without memory, even the most finely written speech may come off as wooden and artificial if the speaker has to stare at the words on a page. Whether addressed in face-to-face contexts or on video, audiences want to feel they are connecting on a personal level with the speaker. Creating this relationship requires memory and delivery to work together in concert.

Memory

The canon of memory remains one of the most important facets of an effective speech for two reasons. For the speaker, memorizing and therefore internalizing a speech provides the level of confidence we normally feel in our casual conversations with others. One of the reasons we do not feel nervous speaking to people during most of the day is the fact that we know what we are going to say and have a reason to say it. When we fail to memorize a speech adequately, we often feel like we are speaking someone else's words and therefore feel awkward and self-conscious. For the audience, hearing a speech that feels like it comes "from the heart" and not from a manuscript or a teleprompter makes the message more powerful and more sincere and therefore creates a much greater feeling of community and participation.

The initial idea of memorizing a speech may sound impossible. However, our anxiety is only because we have false expectations of what it means to commit a speech to memory. In public speaking, "memorization" does not

DOI: 10.4324/9781003316787-3

mean the literal and exact copying of a written text, as if we could "cut and paste" a speech into our mind as we do in a word processor. Not only is exact reproduction out of reach for most people, but most of the time it isn't even desirable. Only formal addresses made from a podium at official events usually demand sticking precisely to a script, and during those events the speaker usually has a physical copy or teleprompter to rely upon. By contrast, in both rhetorical public speaking and digital social influencing, a degree of improvisation makes a speech feel more intimate and personal. For these situations, committing a speech to memory means knowing the content and the order of key parts of the speech while allowing our natural conversational instincts to fill in the gaps and transitions.

The method that became synonymous with the canon of memory in the classical world was the method of *loci*, which in Latin meant "places." It is from the method of *loci* that the signposting tactic of saying "in the first place" and "in the second place" originated. Various authors subsequently have called the method of *loci* a "memory journey," a "mental map," or a "mind palace." This book will use the term **mind palace** to refer to a device used to commit a large amount of information to memory by combining visual and spatial memory. A mind palace is not a physical location, but an imagined (but familiar) space you build in your mind and populate with visual reminders of key parts of your speech. As you progress through your speech, you then travel through this palace room by room, taking note of what you have placed in each location. Although this technique may initially strike professional speakers as almost childlike, it has been around for over two thousand years and was employed by many of the great orators from Demosthenes to Cicero. You cannot argue with success.

The following are the proven techniques of the mind palace:

1   *Generate an inventory.* Read your speech as if you were taking an **inventory**, meaning a count of all of the essential items in the speech, including such things as the main ideas, quotations, facts, narratives, arguments, and examples. Write down each of these and give each of them a name that is unique to the item. For instance, "fishing story" or "cancer definition" or "Mayo Clinic doctor" or "Obama foreign policy" or "the Golden Rule." When you name each item, make sure the name you choose is as concrete as possible. Then hand write this inventory in the order it appears in your speech, as handwriting helps retain the memory of what you write better than a computer.

2   *Find your palace.* Your **palace** provides the map you will use to construct your blueprint. As a guide for this map, find a place with which you are intimately familiar and that hold a variety of rooms, buildings, paths, and unique spaces. A palace need not be a literal building. Certainly, the layout of one's childhood home would work perfectly. But so would one's neighborhood, a city block, a nature path, or university campus. What is essential for a mind palace is the ability to diagram a space in one mind and

be able to move about inside of that space without effort. Choose a palace whose size and complexity matches the length of your inventory.

3   *Draw your blueprint.* Take a blank piece of printer paper and literally draw the **blueprint** for your palace, which is the two-dimensional representation of the space. Focus on walls, doors, paths, and other key spaces. Use different colors and idiosyncratic details to give your map character and even a sense of humor. The more enjoyable the process in making the map, the more your mind will be imprinted with its design.

4   *Plan your route.* Looking at your blueprint, now plan a **route** through your mind palace, which is the continuous path you will take through its rooms, hallways, roads, or paths. Literally draw this route in a continuous, curving line through the palace, making the beginning and endpoints with an appropriate symbol. Each **storage space** along the route should represent a place where you will locate parts of your inventory. These storage spaces should be literal places, such as on a floor or table, inside a cabinet, on top of a shelf, on an exercise bike, at a desk, or beside a window. Try to group parts of the speech that appear together under main ideas within separate places. For instance, the storage spaces of the introduction may all be located around the front porch, whereas the arguments for the first main point are in the living room. Make sure there are just enough places to match your inventory, no more and no less. In your mind, walk through this route several times and imagine you passing through it in three-dimensional space.

5   *Translate your inventory into symbols.* This step is the most creative and important in the method of a mind palace. You cannot simply store exact facts, names, numbers, or quotes in your mind palace and have them stick around. You first have to translate them into vivid **symbols** which (a) have some relationship to the information, (b) are easy to recall, and (c) are unusual, catchy, surprising, clever, or funny. Perhaps you are giving a speech on Abraham Lincoln's Gettysburg address. One might imagine a baseball player wearing Lincoln's hat, telling you they won the game by the score of four to seven. Hence, "Four score and seven years ago." If you are telling a story of the time you first went fishing with a parent, place the shark from the movie *Jaws* or the fish from *Finding Nemo*. Use color to symbolize emotion, like red or blue for anger or sadness. Change the size of your objects to represent magnitude. Use the first letter of each object to create an acronym. The possible combinations are unlimited. Whatever aids in recall will work.

6   *Fill your mind palace with symbols.* Now walk through your **blueprint** and place the **symbols** of your **inventory** along the **route** into each **storage space**. Don't overfill each space. In each room, you should only have as many symbols as you can visualize in one mental image. If any one place becomes too cluttered, it will not work as a guide. Using your physical map, draw each symbol in its appropriate storage space, ideally using different colors. Now mentally retrace the route, carefully

seeing each symbol in each space without thinking too hard about what it represents.

7   *Practice recalling the inventory room by room.* After you have become comfortable in your mind palace, knowing exactly where each symbol is located along the route, walk through the palace again and practice translating the symbols back into the information of your inventory. Do this in sections first. Take one room at a time and walk through it until it becomes effortless. Now move to the next room. Once you master each room, put the entire speech together.

8   *Read the speech out loud.* When we read to ourselves silently our minds and bodies are not preparing themselves to perform the text out loud. We read silently to absorb information and to process it, not to memorize it and reproduce it. An essential component of memorization is reading this speech out loud and in a strong voice that fills the room. Whispering to oneself on the bus will not produce a confident speech. One must find a private place in which one can hear one's own voice.

9   *Practice with your whole body.* Do not practice a speech by sitting in a chair. Use your entire body. Walk around the room (ideally the room where you will be speaking) and use gestures as you speak to an imaginary audience. The more your body becomes engaged in the speech act, the more your mind becomes engaged as well. Treat your body as a partner in the speech and it will help you.

10 *Record and listen to yourself.* Listening to your own voice not only helps you improve delivery by hearing your own voice as an audience would hear it; it also improves memory by externalizing your voice and making you encounter it as you might encounter popular song lyrics.

11 *Take breaks.* Relying on one extended practice session is generally not sufficient for good memorization. Memory needs time to filter out what is important and then to solidify long-term memory by continually returning to the same thing. Taking breaks for a couple of hours, during which time you do nothing that is related to the speech, is often very helpful in retention. Memorization is a process, not a one-time event. The brain generates memory through the repetitions that create stable neural pathways.

The canon of memory, in short, is the act of absorbing the content and form of the speech so fully into oneself that the speech feels like an unforced expression of one's thoughts and feelings. Therefore, as a canon, memory remains a crucial component of a speech even when reading from a manuscript or from cue cards. Anyone who has attended a formal event can tell you how excruciating it is to hear people reading from manuscripts that they have not rehearsed. The canon of memory tells us that it is not enough to simply deliver words in the correct order; one has to feel what is being said and to deliver it with a sense of intimacy and passion. In a broad sense, then, memory should be considered essential to all forms of effective delivery.

Delivery

The canon of delivery addresses the way a speech is actually performed with the body. Although conceptually the simplest of the canons, it perhaps is the most difficult to master and requires a great deal of training and experience before an audience. It also is one of the most important because it gives to a speech its life and passion. Ralph Waldo Emerson provides the following encomium to deliver in his essay "Eloquence," focusing specifically on the importance of voice:

> A good voice has a charm in speech as in song; sometimes of itself enchains attention, and indicates a rare sensibility, especially when trained to wield all its powers. The voice, like the face, betrays the nature and disposition, and soon indicates what is the range of the speaker's mind … Every one of us has at some time been the victim of a well-toned and cunning voice, and perhaps been repelled once for all by a harsh, mechanical speaker. The voice, indeed, is a delicate index of the state of mind. I have heard an eminent preacher say that he learns from the first tones of his voice on a Sunday morning whether he is to have a successful day. A singer cares little for the words of the song; he will make any words glorious.[1]

For Emerson, not only can delivery undermine even the most carefully crafted composition, but it can also turn ordinary ideas into a glorious oration. Delivery has this power because of the unique capacity of the human voice to portray what Emerson refers to as the "nature and disposition" of the speaker. We are naturally drawn to people who speak with confidence and grace and power, trusting that the ideas contained within the language match the character and virtue conveyed through voice and stature.

The first four qualities of delivery relate to the appearance of a speaker and how he or she relates to an audience in terms of their physical body. Appearance, gesture, position, and eye contact can be practiced in front of a mirror to get a sense of how one looks from the other side. The last seven qualities of delivery have to do with the sound of one's voice. Articulation, pronunciation, dialect, pitch, volume, pauses and rate should be practiced by listening to one's own voice on an audio recording. It is an interesting phenomenon of media that we do not mind looking at pictures of ourselves, but we cannot stand listening to recordings of ourselves. Nonetheless, recording oneself speaking and listening to it (especially without video accompaniment) can produce a great deal of improvement in our public speaking. The fact is that the sound of people's voices matter. We gain a lot of information from sound that extends beyond the delivery of information.

---

1   Ralph Waldo Emerson, "Eloquence," available at https://emersoncentral.com/essays/eloquence (accessed March 24, 2022)

Sound creates emphasis and conveys emotion as well as aids in memory and understanding.

Although it is important to consider each of the following elements of delivery individually, when actually performing the speech, one should think of delivery as a coherent whole. One should consider how different acting styles dramatically alter the way that an audience interprets the language of a character. Just as different actors bring different elements to the same character, different delivery styles alter the way the same speech text is received. Consequently, one should think of an oratorical rostrum as a kind of stage in which one steps into a certain "role" or "character." Rather than isolating each of the elements of delivery and building them up into a unity, one should simply think of certain familiar performance styles and imitate them as best one can. Not only does this method provide a coherent delivery style to imitate, but it also puts speakers into a performative frame of mind that relieves the anxiety of feeling as if they have to "be themselves." The fact is that when people are delivering public speeches, the last thing they should do is act like they always act in everyday life. A speech is a performance and should be treated as such. Indeed, it is not infrequent that people who are quiet or reserved in everyday conversation turn out to be the best public speakers. As Emerson says, "The most hard-fisted, disagreeably restless, thought-paralyzing companion sometimes turns out in a public assembly to be a fluent, various and effective orator."[2] The stage can be liberating for those who know it is a performance.

Lastly, delivery does not simply entail physical skill; it also has a cognitive and emotional component insofar as it grows out of three kinds of knowledge. First, you should *know your audience*. When we know our audience, we instinctively adapt our manner of speaking to their personalities and expectations, most notably in our level of formality but also in many other subtle aspects, including our rate of speaking, our volume, our level of animation, our use of humor, and our incorporation of slang terms or jargon. Knowing something about the audience ahead of time allows us to develop a presentation style adapted to their attitudes. Second, you should *know the speaking environment*. Find a time to familiarize yourself with where you are speaking. The serves several purposes: (a) knowing the environment simply makes you feel more at home; (b) if the speech is to be amplified, testing equipment makes the speaker accustomed to the sound of your own voice; and (c) standing at the rostrum (or equivalent) allows you to know where the audience will be sitting, where you can move while speaking, and what physical elements of the environment might be useful to incorporate into a speech in passing reference. Third, you should *know what you want to say*. By this, I do not simply mean what words you are saying. I mean you should believe in what you are saying and feel confident in your

---

2   Ralph Waldo Emerson, "Eloquence," available at https://emersoncentral.com/essays/eloquence (accessed March 24, 2022)

message. Delivery is a natural outgrowth of enthusiasm, and enthusiasm is difficult to fake. No matter how charismatic and charming a person is in their everyday interactions, no natural charisma can overcome a lack of preparation and purpose.

1 *Appearance.* One's appearance means how a speaker dresses and physically presents him- or herself in terms of grooming, fashion, and posture. The function of **appearance** is not only to please the eye but also to identify oneself to an audience as a certain type of person who will deliver the message in a certain type of way. Our outward appearance can thus be considered a kind of "sign" of what is to come and a "promise" of what the audience should expect. It makes a big difference, for instance, whether one delivers a board-room speech in a business suit or whether one delivers a speech in a swimsuit. In both cases, one might deliver the same exact address, but in the first case be taken seriously and in the second case be interpreted as a source of comedy. But if one were giving a toast to a friend at a beach party, the exact opposite would be true and the person with the business suit would be thrown into the ocean. In short, the important thing to consider with appearance is the setting of the speech and the audience who will be receiving it. Our appearance is a way of establishing a relationship with an audience and giving them a visible sign of what is to come before you even say a word.

2 *Gesture.* When we use **gestures** we mostly use our arms, hands, and face to convey nonverbal meanings. There are three primary functions of gesture. First, a gesture may have a meaning unto itself and condense complex meanings into simple and powerful movements. An upraised fist, hands placed in prayer, arms spread wide, fingers clasped together, all of these are typical gestures which in particular cultures have very specific meanings and can be used to take the place of words. Second, gestures provide a visual reinforcement of the words that are being said. For instance, in saying "let us all come together" it would be appropriate to move your hand slowly together until your fingers are intertwined. Gestures create a more visible performance akin to an actor on a stage that not only conveys a deeper and more artistic sense of meaning, but also makes the speaker more interesting to look at and concentrates attention not just on their voice but on their whole person. Lastly, gestures can literally demonstrate how something looked or happened, as when we might use gestures to show the size and shape and placement of objects, the way a room was laid out, the way a person behaved or acted, and the like. In this sense, gestures are kind of like a game of charades. This kind of effect can actually be very powerful on an audience, as it puts them at ease and gives them something specific to watch.

3   *Position.* A speaker's **position** refers to how a speaker orients his or her body with respect to the audience, including the choice of whether to stand behind a podium, walk around, or sit down. The function of position is to develop a certain relationship to an audience and to the environment in which one is speaking. In general, one can distinguish between formal and informal positioning. A formal style will often be behind a podium or on a raised rostrum or in front of a long table, in which case one is expected to adopt a more direct lecture style of presentation in which one is in "command" of the room. Such a position is intended to convey authority and focus attention on the speaker often at the expense of the audience. An informal style will usually be in a smaller setting with a more scattered or circular seating arrangement that offers room to move around and engage individuals directly in the audience. In this case, the speaker has a more relaxed posture and often engages in a give-and-take with the audience, sometimes directly approaching them in the manner as one would talk to a friend. Even on video, a position close or far away from the camera conveys a sense of intimacy or detachment, even though it is completely simulated. Sometimes, in fact, a speaker can alternate between different distances to emphasize specific messages.

4   *Eye contact.* One of the most important predictors of the impact of the speech is the degree to which a speaker has **eye contact** and looks at members of the audience while speaking. Merely glancing at the audience during moments of silence does not constitute eye contact. Ideally, one must "look" as if one is having a conversation with somebody. The function of eye contact is to create a relationship with the audience and make them feel as if the speaker is directly talking *with* them rather than simply talking *at* them. In addition, eye contact lets an audience know that the speaker is paying attention to them and is interested in their opinions and feedback. When a speaker does not look at the audience, an audience often drifts away and treats a speaker more as a recording than as an individual. Eye contact encourages an audience to treat the speaker as an individual. In turn, when the audience feels they are being directly engaged, they often generate more feedback that can help the speaker adapt to their nonverbal expressions and attitudes. Clearly, good eye contact relies upon at least partial success in mastering the techniques of memory. Even when performing a speech on video using shorter scenes, eye contact matters. Because the audience is watching a close-up of the speaker on the screen, reading from notecards or a computer is obvious to a viewer and even less forgivable because of the medium.

5   *Articulation.* One way public speaking differs from conversation is that there is far more attention paid to how distinctly one uses **articulation**, so that each letter distinctly stands out, as in pronouncing the word ar-TIC-u-LA-tion with hard syllables and a sense of rhythm. The opposite of articulation is mumbling. The function of articulation is twofold.

First, it serves the purpose of making each word distinct so that people are able to understand exactly what is being said. A missed word or a phrase that blends together often creates confusion and forces the audience to try to figure out what was said after the fact. This often leads to an audience being distracted. Second, articulating words conveys the impression that each word is meaningful and deserves attention. In this case the effect is similar to how one might think of a staccato note in music that punctuates it and distinguishes it from other notes. Articulating one's words helps an audience remember them because they stand out in their memory.

6   *Pronunciation*. Although we often take this for granted, it is quite important to actually be able to pronounce words. The function of **pronunciation** is not only to accurately convey meaning but to show one's own credibility. It is relatively common, for instance, for candidates for public office to find themselves in an embarrassing new story because they could not pronounce the name of a country, a country's leader, or a word that has particularly significant meaning for a particular demographic. Mispronouncing words is a sign that one has not taken the time to actually figure out what the words mean and how they are used by the people who care about those words.

7   *Dialect*. A **dialect** is a local phrasing common in a particular group but not used universally. "Slang" can be considered a kind of dialect, although one person's slang is another person's cultural vocabulary. Dialect can have a positive and negative effect on a speech. The positive effect of dialect is to either emphasize the unique characteristic of one's heritage to an audience that does not speak in it or to create a sense of identification with an audience that does. The use of dialect requires, of course, that one uses and pronounces it correctly. This leads to the negative effect of trying to use dialect, in which case it either alienates an audience to whom it is unfamiliar or, if misused, embarrasses oneself before an audience familiar with the dialect.

8   *Pitch*. The first type of sound is **pitch**, a musical term that refers to the ability to speak each word as if it was a separate note in a melody, moving up and down the scale. When we turn up our voice at the end of the question, for instance, what we are doing is raising the pitch. Or when we make a declaration we often go down at the end of our statement in order to convey that we have come to a rest. So the best way to think about the function of pitch is to create an alternation of tensions and resolutions which often accompanies specific emotional qualities such as excitement, warning, frustration, fear, happiness, or relief. Indeed, the same sentence spoken with different pitch can often connote a completely different meaning, as for instance the difference between being serious and sarcastic. One of the consistent problems in public speakers is the tendency to keep a monotone pitch throughout a sentence and only to drop it at the end of a sentence. Pitch, however,

should move either up or down in the middle of a sentence, not simply at the end. Choose specific words in a speech to mark as moving up or down, often with up or down arrows marked next to them. Think of pitch as a musical score.

9   *Volume.* The dynamic between softly and stridently spoken parts of the speech is **volume**. Of course, the essential part of volume is simply to speak loud enough so that you can be understood by the entire room. Oftentimes we overestimate the loudness of our voice. When we speak without microphones to an average size room, we often require raising the volume of our voices beyond our normal speaking voice. However, one should avoid a volume so high that it appears that one is shouting at the audience. But volume can also be used for effects within the speech. A quieter voice communicates either suspense or caution or sympathy, whereas a louder voice communicates excitement or warning or confidence. An effective speech should always have softer and louder sections much as one would think of a symphony going through many acts. Lastly, one should think about volume in terms of how much participation you wish from your audience. The lower your voice is, the more that an audience has to "lean in" to understand what is being said. The higher one voice is, the more they sit back and simply listen to you without making any effort. Requiring too much effort might make them lose interest, whereas not requiring enough effort might make them seek to pay attention. Generally speaking, we can speak quieter when we know we have an audience's attention, whereas we speak loudly when we want to get their attention.

10 *Pauses.* Sometimes using **pauses** in a speech, which is adding a patient and conscious silence between words or thoughts, generates a great deal of energy. A pause is important especially for creating tension or suspense as well as for giving the audience a time to think or reflect for a few seconds. Particularly when one is making a grave or important point, pauses allow us to emphasize those key parts of the speech which you want the audience to pay special attention to. Generally, a speech should try to work in two or three distinct pauses for this reason.

11 *Rate.* The dynamic between rapidly and slowly spoken parts of the speech is **rate**. For the most part, we speak rapidly during parts of the speech that do not require a great deal of intellectual processing but are mainly to communicate simple ideas and generate enthusiasm in an audience. The passages are also often spoken with a higher volume. Slower parts of the speech are meant to convey ideas that require either more intellectual reflection or a greater depth of emotional understanding. Sometimes these lower passages are spoken with a softer voice as well, as we wish the audience to participate in the moment in a thoughtful way. However, slow passages can also be spoken with great volume when they wish to hammer home a very specific point.

Delivery Form

The delivery form refers to the degree to which you will rely on memory aids (if any) when delivering a speech. The choice of how you will deliver your speech has important consequences for how it will be received by an audience, quite apart from what is said. Using a manuscript shows both extensive preparation as well as an inflexibility in performance, whereas an impromptu speech displays confidence and informality while promising a less polished and more conversational tone. The choice also opens up and limits certain possibilities for how a speech will be written, how much information it will contain, and how long it will be. The following are the four choices for the delivery form.

1   *Manuscript.* Reading from a manuscript means writing out every word of a speech and delivering it as written. Except in cases with a tele-prompter, the manuscript should be on a podium and the speaker should have practiced the speech to the extent that much of it has been partially memorized. This allows a speaker to look down briefly to keep his or her place but still maintain eye contact with an audience. In this regard, it is helpful to write marks on the speech for when to breathe (~), when to look up (↑), and when to look back down (↓) so that you can memorize sections that you think warrant a more significant delivery. Manuscript reading allows for a careful sculpting of stylistic language (in the cases of commemorative speaking) or complex arguments (in deliberative speaking) that would otherwise be difficult to convey. Manuscripts are most proper for formal occasions in which the audience expects and demands this kind of complexity and subtlety. However, manuscript may provide a "crutch" that speakers rely on too much, which causes them to effectively ignore the audience and deliver the speech as if they were simply reading out loud.[3]

2   *Impromptu.* Delivering **impromptu** speeches means to speak without preparation on a subject given to you at the moment. This form is the most natural and spontaneous and thus often the most interesting to hear. However, it also limits one's ability to sculpt a careful argument and provides no safety net should one run out of ideas. We engage in impromptu speaking all the time in social events when we feel we have to impress or entertain a listener we just met. Impromptu speaking may be required during deliberative meetings, such as in the boardroom, the town hall, or the family kitchen, and also during celebratory occasions in which people are called upon to make a speech about themselves or others. Successful impromptu speaking requires a speaker to come up with a topic and stick to it, crafting two or more coherent main points and defending them using memories, common sense facts, and other examples ready to hand.

---

3   See James C. Humes, *Talk Your Way to the Top* (New York: McGraw-Hill, 1980).

3   *Extemporaneous.* The essential feature of **extemporaneous** speaking is the notecard, which includes key points, quotes, and transitions drawn from a larger outline but leaves the speaker to fill in the gaps during the actual delivery of the speech. This form provides structure but allows for adaptation in such a way that, ideally, the speaker will be able to connect with the audience on a personal level while still making a formal argument or presentation. A good notecard will thus be easy to read, will not be cluttered with information, and will support the speech by providing both information and delivery instructions, such as when to look up, when to make a gesture, when to speak loudly, and when to slow down. Extemporaneous speeches are ideal for people making "official" presentations in front audience members who feel free to break in and ask questions at any time. The speaker is able to deal with such interruptions because he or she still has all the important information directly at hand, and he or she can flip backward and forward without completely disrupting the flow of the speech.

4   *Memory.* Delivering from **memory** is to compose a speech and then rehearse it until one knows it by heart. At its best, it has all the advantages of manuscript style without the disadvantages, for it allows a speaker to engage an audience directly and to walk around a "stage" without being tied to a podium. However, speeches from memory also put one at great risk. If one forgets even the smallest part of a speech, there is the danger that one's mind might go blank like that of an actor in a play, at which point there is nothing to help the speaker find his or her place. In addition, relying on memory makes it hard if not impossible to adapt to an audience during the speech, such as when external interference occurs or when a speaker simply realizes that something isn't working. For most people, speeches from memory are thus best when they are short and have only a few simple points, such as a wedding toast or an argument in a public meeting. They also are excellent for storytelling exercises, as stories are easier to remember, and audiences enjoy hearing stories from people as if they simply sprung naturally from memory.

Visual Aids

A **visual aid** supplements the verbal component of a speech with graphic displays intended to effectively condense complex material or to convey meanings that cannot be captured with language itself. Visual aids are different from visual rhetoric. In visual rhetoric, the image is the form of persuasion itself—as in a billboard, a political cartoon, or an iconic photograph. A visual aid, by contrast, complements the written or spoken words by supplying an image that more effectively conveys a specific idea, represents a specific fact, or portrays a dramatic example. Such aids include the bar graphs and tables of speech of administration, the personal objects often used in introductory speeches, the graphic images and statistics used in speeches of advocacy to dramatize problems, and the photographs or symbols useful in commemorative speeches in stimulating memory and emotion.

Visual aids thus perform two major functions. First, they simplify complex information that otherwise could not effectively be explained. Second, they graphically visualize an event, object, person, or process whose details are necessary for understanding a speech. To be effective, visual aids should be large enough to see and colorful and interesting enough to capture an audience's attention. However, more is not necessarily better. We are often so inundated with visual images that we often assume that we should always try to use as many visual aids as possible. But as a general rule, visual aids should be kept to a minimum and should never be forced into a speech simply to "dress it up" if there is no reason for them to be there. If a good description can describe something with eloquence, then a picture of that event does not "add" to the speech. It replaces or competes with it. Visual aids should never be in competition with the speaker or the speech. Whenever a visual aid takes attention away from the speech itself, it has failed in its purpose as an *aid*. In other words, a visual aid should be used to supplement a speech by performing a task that only a visual aid can perform. The following are examples of useful visual aids:

1 *Bullet-point lists* to summarize the main points of the speech.
2 *Quotations* to show the words used by Lincoln during the Gettysburg Address.
3 *Videos* to reveal what occurred at different stages of a street protest.
4 *Bar graphs* to compare the infection rates of COVID-19 across different countries.
5 *Line graphs* to show the growth and decline of a nation's manufacturing over a decade.
6 *Pie charts* to show the different percentage of majors at a university.
7 *Maps* to show where the effects of rising sea levels might affect populations.
8 *Representations* to show how a bump-stock functions in a semi-automatic weapon.
9 *Flowcharts* to show the steps for the passage of a law through Congress.
10 *Photographs* to show the different fashion trends of the 1980s.
11 *Chalkboard drawings* to show the process of solving a math problem.
12 *Handouts* to provide an audience with the specific language of a proposed law.
13 *Objects* to demonstrate the different pieces of equipment used in mountain climbing.
14 *Poster boards* to display the methods, findings, and conclusions of a journal article.

Although each of these visual aids has its own unique form, they all share one quality common to any visual aid. They all objectify information. In other words, each of them extracts some information from the speech, represent it through a simplified visual form, and present that information as if it had an independent existence. It is important to recognize this function because it has both advantages and disadvantages. The advantage is that it captures information in a permanent form that allows an audience to carefully examine it independent from the words of the speaker. A chart, photo, map, or quotation can all be viewed, read, interpreted, and analyzed on its own. This gives the audience the opportunity to develop their own judgments, better understand the information, and participate in the construction of meaning. The disadvantage is that its very independence means the visual aid can compete for attention. A striking photograph, for instance, might so engage an audience that it stops paying close attention to the words of the speaker. Quotations invite an audience to read them carefully, which creates two competing scripts in their consciousness. When developing a visual aid, therefore, it is important to maximize its advantages and reduce its disadvantages.

One of the positive aspects of **digital social influencing** is that it can effectively eliminate the distraction and competition of visual aids through careful editing. As mentioned in Chapter 2, visual aids used on video can be inserted directly on the screen below, above, or to the side of the speaker for a short amount of time. (Only fill the screen with a visual aid and use a voiceover effect when absolutely necessary.) In addition, due to the possibility that a video can simply be played back or paused, these visual aids need not be on the screen for a long period of time. Indeed, sometimes in video productions, visual aids can last for only seconds at a time and appear in rapid procession. In a face-to-face context, this kind of presentation would seem chaotic. But on video, one can make use of a far quicker presentation style. In many ways, in fact, a speech that requires extensive visual aids often might benefit from a digital presentation.

The greater challenge in usual visual aids comes in **rhetorical public speaking** before a live audience. One clear benefit of a face-to-face speech is that it offers the ability to use physical objects, such as handouts, objects, chalkboards, or samples, that have a unique tactile quality. Only in a shared speech setting can one sample a glass of wine or hold an ancient Roman coin. But for the rest of these visual aids, the clear challenge is to use visual aids in a way that doesn't compete with or distract from a speech. Today, visual aids are almost exclusively displayed using a projector that displays the contents of a computer onto a screen. Furthermore, the visual aids are compiled using some form of digital slideshow such as PowerPoint. Especially for speeches that deal with technical, legal, scientific, or economic subject matter, having constant visual aids throughout the speech, without interruption, has become the norm. There are good reasons for this trend. Analyzing the profits and losses of a company for the past year requires sophisticated graphs to show trends, while scientific papers that have sifted through hundreds if not thousands of data points can only be understood using visual aids.

As necessary as visual aids are to specific types of speeches, they can be overused and used badly. One of the biggest mistakes people make when using these sorts of presentations is that the person speaking makes themselves virtually supplementary to the actual presentation. This can occur when people put up all of their information onto the screen so that the audience tends to simply read the screen rather than listen to or watch the speaker. The effect of making oneself a mere "supplement" to the visual presentation is made worse when the person speaks in a dark room and stands off into a corner behind a podium reading from a manuscript without looking at an audience, thus creating the effect that the audience are just listening to a voiceover of a slideshow. None of these things lead to an effective presentation. No matter the complexity of the topic, you should never assume that an audience has gathered together simply to see images on a screen. They are there to hear what you have to say about those images.

The following are guidelines on how to effectively use visual aids in face-to-face settings.

1   *Position yourself to be seen by an audience.* When possible, stand rather than sit and make use of a lavalier microphone. Concentrate on making yourself the center of the presentation by standing in such a way that it draws attention to yourself without blocking the screen. Avoid standing below or directly to the side of a screen, especially when that area is dark. Also, do not stand directly between the projector and the screen so that you have light cast on your face while casting a shadow behind you. Then you are an obstruction. Ideally, find a space in front and slightly off the side of the projector screen that allows you to gesture both toward the audience and behind you toward the visual aids. Carry a tablet or smartphone in one hand, if necessary, to manage the presentation.

2   *Talk to the audience, not to a computer screen.* Even when you must stay seated or are restricted to standing behind a podium, do not use this as an excuse to stare at the computer display and read your script and/or interpret your visual aids straight off of the computer. Commit your major, non-technical points to memory and speak directly to your audience using eye contact. When you do refer to your visual aids, your eyes should be looking not at your computer display but the projector screen like the rest of your audience. By looking at the same source of information, you help direct their attention and also create a feeling of participation and engagement.

3   *Use a clicker with a laser pointer.* Liberate yourself from the computer keyboard by using a Bluetooth clicker to advance the slides from a standing position. Doing this in the midst of your speech creates a feeling that the slideshow is an extension of your speech rather than a separate presentation. Advance the slides while you are talking directly to the audience rather than pausing and turning your back on the audience. A laser pointer can also assist in engaging directly with the

material and focusing audience attention on specific facets of the visual aid that is relevant to your current idea.

4   *Keep some lights on.* If you are using a projector screen, do not throw the entire room in the darkness. This reproduces the feeling of a theater and makes the screen, rather than the speaker, the focus on attention. When you speak from a shadowy corner, especially when you are wearing a microphone, you give the impression of simply being a voiceover recording of a video presentation and the speech loses its personal touch. In addition, dark rooms tend to make people sleepy. Instead, dim the lights immediately near the screen, but keep others lights on and stand in a brighter spot in the room.

5   *Only represent essential information on your slides.* Whenever possible, let your speech do the hard work of communicating the key ideas, arguments, and conclusions. Visual aids should not be used to reproduce or summarize your speech. Worse still, visual aids should not overwhelm an audience with data or reveal your arguments before you make them. Each image should clearly represent one or two key elements of your speech, and should be restricted to presenting only that information that requires visual representation. Ideally, a slide should present information that raises a question that you answer in your speech. Encourage an audience to listen to your words for the answer to a problem or the conclusion to a line of reasoning. If necessary, only display repeat key conclusions *after* you have explained them, using a slide to summarize results.

6   *Use attractive templates.* All slide presentation programs now come with templates that offer attractive colors and designs that make them easy on the eyes. Take advantage of these templates. Avoid simply putting black letters on a white screen. Use color backgrounds that conform to the color palette of the room in which you are presenting.

7   *Use transition slides.* After a visual aid has performed its function in a speech, do not let it stay on the screen after you have moved on to another idea. Then the visual aid actually clashes with the speech itself. Insert transition slides when no visual aid is needed. These slides can simply be a blank template screen in a dark color that does not stand out. You might add very brief text on these screens that acts as a signpost, perhaps announcing the part of the speech, such as "Data" or "Background" or "Discussion" or "Questions." These can act like titles of book chapters.

8   *Make exaggerated gestures.* Actively point to images on the screen as you would using an old-fashioned chalkboard. The more hand or arm gestures and facial expressions you can use while interacting with the board increases your engagement with an audience. Because you are competing with the screen, you need to exaggerate your motions to make yourself seem larger and more animated than the larger image beside you.

9   *Interact with your audience.* Lastly, do not sit back and allow the screen to be the source of interaction between your audience and the speech. Actively engage the audience by asking questions, walking around the

audience, and maintaining eye contact. Again, use position to your advantage. Even if you are confined behind a computer, you can still look up and direct specific comments to members of your audience. Never cower behind technology and use it as an excuse to disappear. Audiences desire interaction.

Speech Anxiety

Almost everyone experiences some level of speech anxiety before and during public speaking. For decades it has ranked among the top three fears that people possess. Something about the social pressure that comes from standing before others and delivering a message makes it seem more terrifying to some people than an immediately physical threat. Compounding the fear of speaking is the embarrassment of the physical effects of speech anxiety, which can include blushing, shaking, sweating, butterflies in the stomach, dry mouth, rapid heartbeat, and squeaky voice. A single bad experience of public speaking, in which our own bodies seemed to betray us, can lead to a lifelong avoidance of the practice and a feeling of being defeated.

Why do we have speech anxiety? The biological answer is that our bodies respond to public speaking as we do in any high stress situation, by releasing adrenaline and activating the "fight or flight" responses of our survival toolkit. From this perspective, speech anxiety may cause us to wish to flee if we feel threatened. But this response can also produce energy that we can channel productively into the speech itself if we can convince ourselves to "fight." The social answer is that for most of us, public speaking is an unusual experience that forces us to take center stage before what we might feel to be a critical audience. The fear of being judged is powerful, especially when we envision ourselves failing before we even begin. Michael Beatty identified eight factors of a speech situation that tend to increase speaking anxiety: the novelty of the speech situation, the formality of the occasion, the subordinate status of the speaker, the degree of conspicuousness felt by the speaker, an unfamiliar environment, the degree of attention from others, the degree to which one is being evaluated, and prior history of bad experiences.[4] When many of these factors come together, a speaker can sometimes feel overwhelmed.

Yet speech anxiety can be overcome. What is important to remember is that although speech anxiety manifests itself as a physiological reaction, it has a psychological cause. For if we look at the act itself, there is nothing terrifying about the actual act of speaking. Composing words and then speaking to them out loud is a completely mundane behavior, especially when done by oneself. What produces anxiety is not the physical act but the mental image of ourselves being observed and judged by others.

---

4   M. J. Beatty, "Situational and Predispositional Correlates of Public Speaking Anxiety," *Communication Education* 37 (1988), 28–39.

Imagine, for instance, a room with a one-way mirror. An individual, thinking they are alone, might be completely at ease even though they are, in fact, being observed. Thus neither the fact of speaking nor the act of being observed generates speech anxiety. It is the perception in the mind of ourselves in that situation that produces anxiety. Consequently, if you can learn to change that mental image, you can literally alter the physical response to the situation.

Below is a list of things to do or keep in mind to deal with speech anxiety:

1 *Know that everyone experiences it.* Speaking anxiety is universal. Even professional speakers get anxious simply because of the fight-or-flight response. Therefore, do not interpret the feeling of anxiety as an indication that you are unprepared. To the contrary, it is an indication that your body is preparing itself to act.

2 *Use nervousness to your advantage.* The energy produced by anxiety can heighten our senses and increase our energy. Instead of trying to suppress this energy, find a way to channel it into the speech through gestures, volume, movement, and passion.

3 *You appear more relaxed than you feel.* Even the most visible signs of anxiety are usually minor when viewed from a distance. Shaking hands or a tremor in the voice may be noticeable, but they usually bother the speaker more than the audience. Therefore the best way to overcome these physiological responses is simply to ignore them. Once the initial rush of energy passes, they typically subside in a short time.

4 *The audience is usually on your side.* With rare political exceptions, people do not attend speeches to watch people fail. They attend speeches to listen to people they find interesting. Hence, the audience will almost always wish for a speaker to do well. Remind yourself that even if you make a mistake, the audience will stay with you. Envisioning the audience as supportive is invaluable to relieving anxiety.

5 *Have something important to say.* Nothing rattles a speaker more than standing up only to find that you don't care about your topic and have written a boring speech. Hastily written speeches made simply to "get it over with" are frequently the causes of speaking anxiety because one starts judging one's own speech as a failure. Taking the time to say something you want to say makes speaking a much more pleasurable experience. Therefore make sure you choose a topic that reflects your actual commitments.

6 *Visualize success.* Like almost any coach in competitive sports will tell you, if you focus on the little things, you will get so caught up in minutiae that you lose sight of the "big picture." As simplistic as it sounds, sometimes success comes from visualizing oneself succeeding. Before the speech, take a moment to close your eyes and quite literally picture yourself speaking successfully as if watching yourself from the audience. Go through the entire speech this way, connecting the words

to your actions. You will find that this visualization generates pathways in the mind that makes performance smoother.

7   *Release tension before speaking.* Purely on a physical note, clenching and then releasing muscles or exerting energy in some way loosens you up and often gets rid of nervousness that has been built up in your muscles. Before walking into class, do short bursts of physical exertion, like pushups, jumping jacks, or running in place. Sometimes, the more absurd the exercise, the more relaxed you feel afterwards.

8   *Be aware of the speech situation.* One of the hardest things for a speaker to deal with is surprise. Make sure that you are aware of all aspects of the speech situation ahead of time. Know your time limit, the size of your audience, the make-up of your audience, what equipment you will have available to you, and any other details that may affect your presentation. Often it is very helpful to go to the room ahead of time and simply stand in the place you are speaking, orienting yourself to the feel of the space.

9   *Practice!* The most important factor in relieving speech anxiety is practicing your speech out loud. Nothing replaces simple practice. Simply knowing the words of a speech is not sufficient for a good performance. You need to feel "at one" with the speech so that your words and actions occur naturally together. Practice until you have memorized the speech and then practice again until you have completely internalized it. Try reading a speech out loud to yourself three times before delivering it to your audience. Reading it "in your head" *is not* the same as reading out loud. Actually verbalizing the words helps your mouth get used to saying the words and your ears get used to hearing them.

10 *Just keep speaking.* The more you speak in public, the easier it will become. We learn by habit, and public speaking can become a habit once you break through the initial fear. Remember, speech anxiety is a psychological effect that is most extreme when the experience is unfamiliar or strange. The more you do it, the more public speaking will seem like an ordinary action. That is why in a public speaking class, you should speak a little bit every day, even if just for 30 seconds. After a few weeks of sharing in this experience, most students find that it becomes second nature.

Conclusion

One of the overall goals of delivery is the creation of what we might call **atmosphere**, or the unique mixture of qualities that pervade a shared space with others. Even digital social influencing communicates a type of atmosphere, however limited in scope. Delivery generates atmosphere by communicating to the members of an audience the type of relationship the speaker wishes to establish with them. Content alone cannot create atmosphere. No matter how serious or light-hearted the subject matter of the speech on its own, relationships are not formed simply by being exposed to linguistic meanings. They are formed between people. Committing parts of the speech to memory communicates that the speaker has taken both the speech and the audience seriously enough to internalize its message so that they can turn attention to the people to whom they are addressing. Attention to delivery then translates these words and images into powerful emotional messages that communicate the attitudes of the speaker and expresses a relationship to an audience. Delivery is that essential medium of connection between two or more people. Without delivery, a speech is just a string of words. If you take care with your delivery, an audience will, in turn, feel that you care for them.

Discussion Questions

1   Think about your favorite speeches delivered by actors in movies. What is it about their delivery that made their speeches so perfect? Find an online clip of the speech and analyze the performance in detail.

2   Do you think that being "authentic" is the same thing as being "spontaneous"? Or do we become more authentic as we practice and rehearse and hear ourselves speaking until we feel we have gotten it right?

3   How does the manner in which we deliver a speech change how it is interpreted and received? Do we often unfairly judge speakers by how they appear, even before they open their mouths? Or do you think this judgment is fair?

4   Do you have any examples of past speech anxiety that you have had but have overcome? Take the opportunity to share different experiences in order to help give confidence to others.

5   Think of different styles of talk show hosts you see on television. How do they alter their positions based on the type of interaction and performances they are doing?

6   What actors are famous for their vocal performance? Find clips of these actors and discuss what makes their speech patterns unique. Try to imitate them.

7   What types of experiences tend to evoke memories for you? Think of specific objects, events, or sensations that spark these memories in order to understand the process.

Exercises

1   **Script reading**: Find a popular scene in a movie or television where you can find an excerpt from the script. Divide the class into groups, where each student can perform one role in one scene. With the script in hand, perform each scene as dramatically as you can, intentionally exaggerating words and actions.

2 **Performance of literature**: Find a short excerpt from one your favorite books. Practice delivering this excerpt using all of the techniques of delivery. You may bring in a copy of the excerpt if necessary, but focus on eye contract, gestures, and the sound of your voice to evoke passion.

3 **Mind palace**: As a class, find a specific location with which everyone is familiar. Sketch a map of that palace on the board. Now, as a class, compose a speech with at least three pain points, with examples and facts, why smartphones are destroying our memories. Follow all the steps of filling the palace with items. Then ask for volunteers to see who can recite the speech from memory without looking at the board.

References

Beatty, M. J. "Situational and Predispositional Correlates of Public Speaking Anxiety," *Communication Education* 37 (1988), 28–39.

Emerson, Ralph Waldo. "Eloquence," available at https://emersoncentral.com/essays/eloquence (accessed March 24, 2022)

Humes, James C. *Talk Your Way to the Top* (New York: McGraw-Hill, 1980).

4 Invention

Rhetoric is an art of invention. Derived from the Latin word *invenire*, "to find," **invention** is the act of finding something to say that lends support to the speaker's position. Invention provides a public speaker with the resources and knowledge that gives a speech its substance and value. As a method, it refers not only to the *type* of resources that might be helpful but also instructions concerning how to *find* them. Invention therefore might be thought of as the act of gathering things from different receptacles and spreading them out together on a table. The canon of arrangement then looks at this collection and organizes it into a coherent form. As the creative work of arrangement progresses, some of that material finds a central place in the speech, while other material gathered through invention is made peripheral or not used at all. What is important is not what percentage of possible material is used in a speech, but that the speaker feels confident that what has been gathered together during invention is the best choice of all available options. In other words, the best speakers leave many potential resources on the "cutting room floor" as evidence that they have selected only the most fitting material.

One of the great changes in the art of invention that has occurred in the past few decades is the incredible expansion in the quantity of resources now available at our disposal through the internet and social media. Today, we are virtually deluged with information. Being able to locate interesting facts, quotations, stories, primary resources, statistics, and scientific explanations has never been easier than at the present moment. Even just a few decades ago, many libraries still used card catalogs in order to locate books or magazines that were often long out of date. Today, a virtually infinite amount of data is immediately accessible through a simple search. Paradoxically, however, this vast quantity of resources has not led to a diversity in speeches. In many cases, the opposite is true. Because of our reliance on popular search engines like Google or sites like Wikipedia to filter this overwhelming amount of data, speeches on the same topic end up all looking the same. By relying on technology to do the work of invention, our speeches lack creativity, insight, and the personal touch. Worse still, lazy searches often rely on popular but highly suspect resources that very often are products of propaganda.

DOI: 10.4324/9781003316787-4

The result is a conveyor belt of prepackaged arguments, ideologies, diatribes, explanations, conspiracy theories, and entire speeches that can be simply imitated almost verbatim. This has not only led to an obvious increase in the temptation for plagiarism, but perhaps more pervasively has encouraged imitation rather than creativity. Rather than putting together a variety of different material into a speech that is uniquely one's own, the temptation is simply to take available material and simply rearrange it so that it looks slightly different but is really the words and ideas of someone else. It is contingent upon an ethical public speaker, and also one who wishes to make a genuine expression of individuality, to resist this temptation for mere imitation and to endeavor to make a public speech that is a unique and creative contribution to the art of rhetoric. That goal requires invention.

Resources for Invention

What do the methods of invention help you to find? A resource for invention represents any material you can use to build your main points, exemplify an argument, provide proof of claims, connect to an audience, tell a good story, or delight the hearer. Many of these resources are readily available without external research. For instance, many maxims, narratives, and myths are part of the inheritance of any culture stories in what is known as **public memory,** which represents the storehouse of social knowledge, conventions, public opinions, values, and shared experiences. For example, William West says that the study of public memory privileges "certain types of knowledge, certain values, certain ideas, beliefs, symbols—in short, an entire cultural ethnography—coalesces around the apparently innocuous ability to remember the past. Memory serves as the locus of personal history and individual identity."[1] Public memory represents those memories that are handed down from generation to generation, usually through stories and maxims and rituals that attempt to preserve the past in the present. Finding resources in public memory can often entail little more than conversations with friends, family, or oneself. Other resources, such as facts, statistics, examples, and testimony, requires more careful and sustained research using databases, libraries, search engines, and news sites. Gathering material from each of these categories will provide a wealth of resources from which to draw upon to construct a speech that is complex and powerful.

1   *Maxim.* A **maxim** is a short, pithy statement expressing a general truth or rule of conduct that is commonly accepted by culture and used to justify a variety of beliefs and actions. We often encounter maxims in the form of **proverbs** ("A tree is known by its fruit") and **clichés** ("The early bird catches the worm"). All cultures at all times have made

1   William West, "Memory," in *Encyclopedia of Rhetoric,* ed. Thomas Sloan (Oxford: Oxford University Press, 2001), 483.

use of maxims to bind together a community through shared principles and rules. The key for the speaker is to know which maxims speak to the unique culture of the audience while also being fitting to the situation and the argument. The best type of maxims not only convey generally accepted ideas, but also might be given a creative expression by particular individuals in history (Benjamin Franklin: "We must all hang together or we shall all hang separately"). Maxims thus effectively communicate **social knowledge,** which signifies a culture's conventional wisdom and practical judgment.[2] Maxims of this type thus represent the collective judgments of a social group that are the result of past experience and that guide beliefs and behaviors in future situations. They are very powerful tools for establishing common ground with an audience and are often the best place to start building a speech.

2   *Narrative.* A **narrative** is a dramatic story that is more complex than an example, and that captures and holds the attention of an audience by promising that, through the unfolding of the plot and character, something new and satisfying will be produced at the end. Narratives are excellent ways of conveying complex states of affairs in ways that are meaningful and memorable for an audience. It is important to note that stories are not "irrational" components of speeches that are to be opposed with facts and statistics. Quite the opposite: when faced with competing narratives, an audience must decide which narrative is more "rational" to follow. According to Walter Fisher: "Rationality is determined by the nature of persons as narrative beings—their inherent awareness of *narrative probability*, what constitutes a coherent story, and their constant habit of testing *narrative fidelity*, whether the stories they experience ring true with the stories they know to be true in their lives."[3] In other words, **narrative fidelity** refers to how accurately a narrative represents accepted facts. For instance, news reports of recent events have to have narrative fidelity to be considered reliable. **Narrative probability** refers to the coherence of the narrative as a story, quite apart from whether it happened. A tall tale or fable has narrative probability because what happens to the characters seems probable given the premises of the story, no matter how fantastic those premises might be. The most effective narrative from a rhetorical standpoint should have both high narrative probability *and* high narrative fidelity.

2   Thomas Farrell, "Knowledge, Consensus, and Rhetorical Theory," in *Contemporary Rhetorical Theory: A Reader*, ed. John Louis Lucaites, Celeste Michelle Condit, and Sally Caudill (New York: The Guilford Press, 1999), 147.

3   Walter Fisher, "Narration as a Human Communication Paradigm: The Case of Public Moral Argument," in *Contemporary Rhetorical Theory: A Reader*, ed. John Louis Lucaites, Celeste Michelle Condit, and Sally Caudill (New York: The Guilford Press, 1999), p. 247. See also Walter Fisher, *Human Communication as Narration: Toward a Philosophy of Reason, Value, and Action* (Columbia, SC: University of South Carolina Press, 1987).

The narratives we tell of our common histories have particular power in structuring our social organizations, our self-conceptions, and our relationships with other groups.

3 *Myth*. A **myth** is an emblematic story from the past that captures and expresses both a moral lesson and an understanding of historical origins and destiny of a particular group or nation. Calling something a myth does not necessarily mean that it is false or untrue. It only means that whatever factual truth it does contain has been transformed in such a way to convey a meaning that stands above and beyond its historical veracity. Myths may be attached to *individual* people, such as Rosa Parks refusing to give up her seat on a bus, or to *groups* of people, such as the American myth of Thanksgiving. But almost always a myth deals with the celebration and memorial of specifically human actors to whom we look for exemplary actions, which occurred in the distant past, and which lay the foundations of some organization, practice, or institution. We retell myths as a way of providing a common connection between a diverse group of people who may share a common history or purpose. Myths are specific types of narratives that are self-justifying to an audience that has internalized the story and embraces it without need for evidence. Consequently, myths have a powerful but narrow application to groups that already share a commitment to that story as part of their identity and mission.

4 *Fact*. A **fact** is a condensed empirical claim that tells us about some aspect of the world that we can rely upon to be true. Most of the facts that we know come from everyday experience, such as "heavy objects fall" or "the sun sets at night." These might be considered part of common sense and require no citation. But the facts that make a difference are those that derive from scientific, historical, or archival research and refer to specific aspects of our world that are significant, verifiable, and particular. Facts should be considered the "building blocks" of any speech in so far as they are solid, particular, concrete elements that we can rely upon to support our case. We can therefore "stack up" facts as we would with blocks, building a solid platform that can stand up on its own. The most powerful fact should be easily comprehended, succinctly spoken, and should call up a very specific image in people's minds that guarantees that when they encounter something, they will know exactly what it is and what to expect from it.

5 *Statistic*. **Statistics** are different from facts because they do not deal with specific assertions about concrete objects but are mathematical generalizations that help us make predictions about certain types of objects or events. They do not tell us what something *is* but rather what we can probably *expect* of it. For instance, direct use of numeric facts and statistics is helpful to either show the *percentage* of something ("this percentage of college students are women") or the *probability* of something ("the probability of an earthquake along the West Coast has increased"). Particularly when we are concerned with the outcomes of

our potential judgments, statistics that tell us the likelihood of certain outcomes are very persuasive, provided that the statistics come from respected sources and are not distorted by partisan influences. Facts and statistics often work closely together. For instance, that nicotine is an addictive substance is a fact related to its chemical makeup. However, because everyone reacts to nicotine differently, the level of addiction varies widely according to a person's genetics and habits. Consequently, when it comes to describing how nicotine actually influences a population, one must rely on statistics in terms of what percentage of cigarette users become addicted. A fact says that something is always the case. A statistic says only the likelihood that something will be the case for a certain specific population of things or events.

6   *Testimony*. **Testimony** consists of direct quotations from individuals who can speak with some authority on a certain state of affairs. Testimony can come in various forms. **Lay testimony** derives from ordinary people who have had relevant experience with some issue. Such testimony can prove that something exists or has happened by drawing on the personal experience or it can give a "human touch" to a story by using colorful quotes to exemplify some point. For instance, a prisoner at the Auschwitz concentration camp might testify both to the horrific conditions that existed and provide a vivid description of that terrifying experience. **Expert testimony** comes from individuals who may not have directly experienced something but who know a considerable amount about the subject matter due to extensive research. Such testimony is used to challenge or override competing explanations by appealing to the authority of knowledge. For instance, a historian of the Holocaust might have written a book about concentration camps that can be used to provide broader context. Last, **prestige testimony** comes from famous and well-respected individuals who may have nothing directly to do with an issue but whose words provide inspiration and insight. One might look to poets, novelists, or philosophers who provide general quotes about suffering, violence, and cruelty that are relevant to the subject but not written specifically in response to it.

7   *Example*. An **example** is a description of actual or hypothetical events, people, objects, or processes. Examples help embody an idea or argument in a concrete form so that audiences can "see" what it means and/or that can act as evidence to prove the existence or define the nature of something. Examples can be drawn from newspapers, history, biographies, science, or personal experience. They are crucial in embodying abstract claims within concrete visual images that bring to life the causes and consequences of certain actions and beliefs.[4] **Actual examples** are descriptions of real things that exist or have existed, that

---

4   For more on the persuasive use of examples, see Scott Consigny, "The Rhetorical Example," *Southern Speech Communication Journal* 41 (1976), 121–134.

happen or have happened. The main sources of actual examples are history, the news, personal experience, or science. Actual examples are important for making speeches appear thoroughly researched and backed by evidence rather than simply being expressions of personal opinion. **Fictional examples** are descriptions of events that are only imagined having happened in the past, present, or future. There are two kinds of fictional examples. **Third-person fictional examples** describe the actions of other people using the pronouns of *he, she, it,* or *they.* The most effective third-person examples come from stories taken from literature or other popular forms of art that are commonly known by an audience. **Second-person fictional examples** place the audience in a hypothetical situation that asks them to envision doing something by describing the event using the pronoun "you" to put the audience directly in the scene of action, as in "imagine you were living through the Second World War." Second-person examples usually offer the audience some choice to get them thinking about the problem that the speech then proceeds to address. Fictional examples can be helpful in demonstrating the meaning or significance of an idea or value, while actual examples demonstrate that something has occurred as proof of a fact.

Finding Sources

Although the resources of public memory are a good place to start with a public speech, the majority of your inventional resources should be drawn from active research that helps you discover something new that is persuasive, reliable, and novel. The power of invention in this respect often derives from the integrity and breadth of one's **sources**, which are simply the places, people, or things from which something comes or can be obtained. Finding sources that are respected by your audience is essential to persuading them that you are both informed of the situation and sympathetic to their attitudes and concerns. Except in cases of prestige or lay testimony to provide background narratives or inspiring maxims, most people generally tend to respect the same sources—usually those coming from representatives of some established public or private institution such as a university, a news organization, or government research agency. Particularly when using statistics and testimony, data and quotations from individuals with positions that communicate their authority through easily identifiable titles are the most efficient way of establishing credible facts. Sources include not only the people and institutions you use as authorities, but also the media in which those facts, statistics, and quotations appear.

The use of good sources gives **legitimacy** to a speech, which is the quality of being reasonable, fair, reliable, and trustworthy. In politics, legitimacy supports a leader's right to govern; in public speaking, legitimacy supports a speaker's request to be heard. Legitimacy is something that is earned. No matter how charming or entertaining a speaker might be as a person, their arguments lack legitimacy if they seem unrehearsed, unprepared, or reliance on questionable sources. Just as a law acquires legitimacy by having gone through a lengthy process of democratic procedure, so too does a speech acquire legitimacy by showing how its arguments have been developed only after considerable research. Without legitimacy, a speech is not really an argument; it is simply a social or aesthetic performance. At worst, it is just a waste of time.

Also, it is important to recognize that not all sources are created equal. Especially in an age of social media and readily available information online, there are far more questionable and outright "fake" sources than ever before. News, documentaries, videos, seminars, and entire institutes can be found online that purport to give the facts when in reality they are little more than **propaganda**, which represents a campaign of misinformation used to promote or publicize a particular political cause or point of view in a way that intentionally distorts the facts that contradict that view. In the decades prior to the internet, there existed only a few major sources of news or information on which most people relied upon. Consequently, there was generally a shared understanding of what constituted a trustworthy source. Today, the situation is in many ways reversed. Different groups tend to favor sources that reflect their own opinions, thereby creating what is commonly called an **echo chamber** in which people are only exposed to opinions and facts that already support their judgments. The proliferation of conspiracy theories is often the result. Search engines, too, reflect these biases, promoting sites based on popularity rather than accuracy. Once again, with the vast increase in material available to us at your fingertips, it becomes even more necessary to evaluate your resources carefully and avoid simply quoting a source simply because it agrees with your position.

As with so many aspects of public speaking, it is the audience who ultimately determines the legitimacy of your sources. Yet caution is in order. If you speak to a small audience unified in a certain set of beliefs, it is tempting to simply reflect their own biases in order to flatter them. As the old Greek saying goes, "it is easy to praise Athenians among Athenians." The echo chamber exists for a reason; that is because it is simple, quick, and gratifying. The danger arises when this narrowly targeted message reaches an audience outside of the echo chamber. Today, even face-to-face speeches can be easily recorded and disseminated online. At that point, a speech that was an instant success in the echo chamber becomes the subject of ridicule and criticism outside of it. Therefore, the best way to find sources is to seek out those that have legitimacy not only for the primary and target audiences, but also those secondary audiences that might potentially view the speech. Ask yourself, "would this source still be persuasive and legitimate if it became viral online to a diverse public audience?" Seek out those sources that even those who might disagree with your overall argument might still respect.

Lastly, when using any online database or search engine, it is essential to understand how to do efficient **keyword searches**. First, you should avoid relying on general terms alone, such as "global warming" or "civil rights." These will usually call up only the most obvious and general information that rarely goes beyond common sense information. You should always try to pair general terms with specific terms to narrow the search. Try adding specific names, places, dates, or "catchwords" that will call up more relevant searches— for instance, "climate change carbon capture technology," or "Malcolm X violence social change." Second, once you find one source, you should also scan it for more keywords that might be unique and helpful. Then refine your search using proper names, specific phrases, or technical terms. When you search for a specific wording, put that wording in quotation marks in your search to tell the search engine only to look for words that appear in that exact order. Lastly, always check the bibliographies of articles and books to find new sources. Even if they are not immediately helpful, these new sources might, in turn, cite other articles and books in their own bibliographies that are helpful. In short, do not rely only on the sources that you encounter on a first general search or else your speech will sound dull and repetitious. Usually, it takes at least three rounds of searching, each time narrowing your keywords, until you find sources that are relevant, novel, and interesting.

These are some general considerations about how to go about finding sources:

1   *Unaffiliated websites.* As a rule, independent websites that are not affiliated with a professional institution such as a university, newspaper, or government agency are notoriously unreliable sources for information. When not simply the expression of personal opinion, they are more often than not just extensions of **propaganda** for some political position or ideological interest. However, they can serve a useful function in two ways. First, they can be sources of personal narrative or examples of partisan opinions. If a speech examines, for instance, the competing views on gun control, looking to different advocacy websites can be good sources of perspective. Second, these sources may include citations from more legitimate sources in their arguments. For instance, a gun control website might cite statistics from a research study that itself may be widely respected. You can then trace this citation back to the original and use it in your own speech. Also, you might find keywords and phrases in these websites that you can input back into a search engine to refine your search.

2   *Wikipedia.* When starting any research, Wikipedia has quickly become the first stop for most students. There is nothing wrong with beginning with Wikipedia. Although it relies on user-generated content and can sometimes contain questionable facts and interpretations, for most subjects it provides a relatively good overview of a topic and provides a basic framework of understanding. For general knowledge that does not need citation, Wikipedia can be valuable. However, it should only

be considered a means of familiarizing yourself with a topic before delving into more detailed research. Whenever possible, speakers should get in the habit of looking elsewhere for material for invention. Even here, however, Wikipedia can be helpful, as at the bottom of most entries there are references to primary texts or other official sources to investigate. However, Wikipedia should never be cited as an official source in a speech. It should only be used as an introduction to a topic and an indicator of where to find other sources.

3   *News media.* Even though we still refer to "newspapers," the reality is that most of our resources for news are found on the internet. For our purposes, **news media** includes any publication by either for-profit or non-profit organizations whose primary aim is to gather and disseminate news based on research, investigation, interviews, and reporting. These include traditional newspapers like the *New York Times* and *Wall Street Journal*, magazines like *Time* or *The Atlantic*, public broadcasting like *PBS* or *NPR*, network news like *ABC* or *CBS*, or cable news programs like *CNN* or *FoxNews*. These articles and videos can be found on search engines or on library databases like *LexisNexis*. First, news media are excellent sources for quotations from ordinary people about events of public interest. Nothing livens up a speech better than hearing what everyday people have to say about things that happened to them directly. Second, they provide quotations from various "experts" in a highly condensed and lively form that saves a speaker from having to delve through densely written academic material. Third, they usually provide the necessary facts to understand any issue, thus orienting a speaker to the situation. Fourth, journalistic writing is especially helpful in finding examples to use in introductions and conclusions. However, it is important to keep in mind that any news media can frame their stories in a way that favors certain interpretations over others to the stereotypes of their audiences. A responsible speaker will cross-reference numerous articles from respected news sources to determine which facts are generally reliable.

4   *Books.* As old-fashioned as it might sound, books remain one of the best resources for speech topics. Books written about your subject by respected authors provide a wealth of primary material as well as interpretative resources to help back up your claims. Books by university presses are generally more reliable than books by popular presses, although good sources are ultimately not determined by the publisher but by the writer. For books that appear only in print, a good strategy is to first go to the index to see whether your particular interest is represented by a category entry. Often, a quick index search in a biography or history book will give you a wealth of details that could give your speech character. However, many books are now available online through Google Books. It is generally a good idea to first do a search on Google Books to see if there is any quotable material easily

accessible online before having to spend hours flipping through pages in the library. Although Google Books often only has a small portion of any book accessible to search, a general search for key terms may point the way to authors and publications that you can check out of a library. Especially in a time when unaffiliated websites on the Internet have become most people's sources of information, taking the time to cite an academic book and find a striking quotation can be very effective.

5   *Academic journal articles.* The best electronic database for essays from communication and rhetorical scholars is the Communication Source database, accessed via the EBSCO search engine. Also useful is Academic Search Elite. Go to your library and locate this database and search for key terms as you would on any public search engine. This database includes all the essays from journals such as *Quarterly Journal of Speech* and *Philosophy and Rhetoric*. These usually present a very specific argument about an aspect of your case studies from either a scientific or a theoretical perspective. Even if they may not be directly relevant to your argument, they often provide good models for how to critically analyze objects for the purposes of drawing meaningful conclusions.

6   *Public policy resources.* Documents prepared and distributed by government or public policy research agencies are often very useful when looking for data or analysis on general social conditions that can be measured by some objective standard. There are several useful sites you can use for reliable data on public policy. These include:

a   *ProQuest Congressional*: Provides indexes and abstracts of Congressional committee publications, including hearings, committee prints, reports, documents, and public laws.

b   *Congress.gov*: Bills from the 93rd Congress (1973–1975) to present.

c   *Brookings Institute*: A nonprofit public policy organization that conducts policy research and provides recommendations for policy change.

d   *GovInfo.gov*: Provides bills, laws, government reports, GAO Reports, and Public Papers of the Presidents.

e   *The Pew Research Center*: An independent, non-partisan public opinion research organization that studies attitudes toward politics, the press and public policy issues.

f   *Policy Agendas Project*: Collects and organizes data from various archived sources to trace changes in the national policy agenda and public policy outcomes since the Second World War, including congressional hearings, roll call votes, executive orders, supreme court cases etc.

g   *Harvard Kennedy School Library of Think Tanks*: Compiles a list of links to public policy think tanks.

By the end of your research, you should have compiled enough resources with which to start building a speech. However, at this point, all of these examples, narratives, facts, and other resources may not yet fit together into a coherent whole. They are simply collected, as it were, in a box and dumped out on a table. The next two methods of invention, therefore, provide categories, questions, and approaches that help determine which of these resources are most significant and how they can be organized to begin revealing patterns and ideas.

Documenting Sources

Through the invention process, make sure you keep a careful document of your sources. A simple model is the Modern Language Association (MLA) citation style. Use this in recording your sources in an outline, making sure also to retain the page numbers:

1   *Journal or magazine article*: Paroske, Marcus. "Deliberating International Science Policy Controversies: Uncertainty and AIDS in South Africa." *Quarterly Journal of Speech* 95.2 (2009): 148–170.
2   *Newspaper article*: Mitchell, Gordon. "Scarecrow Missile Defense." *Pittsburgh Post-Gazette* July 8, 2001: E-1.
3   *Book*: Danisch, Robert. *Pragmatism, Democracy and the Necessity of Rhetoric.* Columbia, SC: University of South Carolina Press, 2007. Print.
4   *Book article or chapter*: Keränen, Lisa Belicka. "Girls Who Come to Pieces: Shifting Ideologies of Beauty and Cosmetics Consumption in the *Ladies' Home Journal*, 1900–1920." *Turning the Century: Essays in Media and Cultural Studies.* Ed. Carol A. Stabile. Boulder, CO: Westview Press, 2000. 142–165. Print.
5   *Website*: Furness, Zack. "My Dad Kicked Ass for a Living." *BadSubjects. com.* Oct. 2001. Web.

When citing a source in a written paper or outline, you should put the last name of the author and the page number in parentheses at the end of the sentence where the material was cited. For instance: "(Paroske, 150)." This allows you to avoid accusations of plagiarism and also shows your paper to be well researched and documented.

Topics

The last resource for invention is not a particular "thing" but rather a way of relating things together. These are called "topics of invention" (in Greek, *topoi*, which means "places" or "turns"). **Topics of invention** represent specific ways of placing material into relationships that ideally bring about new questions and new insights. If one imagines all of the previous material for invention spread out on a table, topics represent certain places on the table that make the material look different when placed within their circle, much as placing objects under different microscopes or lenses makes them disclose new characteristics. Alternatively, topics are ways of turning subject matter in different directions in a way that illuminate certain sides of them over others. Topics therefore serve the function of invention by encouraging a rhetor to experiment with different ways of asking questions about the subject matter to find out if anything interesting is produced by the different lenses.

When using topics, the best strategy is to use simple pen and paper. Go through each topic, write out the question it asks, and roughly sketch out possible answers. Make sure to start by writing even the most obvious answers. The act of writing down our thoughts externalizes our ideas and helps us see connections that we might not have made in our imagination. Use lines, grids, shapes, columns, and arrows to organize and relate your subject matter. Circle and underline possible lines of argumentation and cross out those that do not seem useful. After an initial brainstorming session, then start again using only those topics that have potential. Even a few minutes of this exercise will almost always produce fruitful results.

Here are five of the most important topics:

1   *Definition.* When you look at something through the topic of definition, you try to find the **definition** of that thing that captures its essential character that distinguishes it from other things. Definition asks "what is the general nature of this thing?" Definition thus shifts the audience's attention from the **particular** (or the concrete, specific, and unique thing) to the **general** (which is the category to which that particular thing belongs). For instance, a discussion of a particular Civil War battle might, through definition, lead one to General Sherman's famous definition that "war is hell," a definition which encompasses all wars for all time. A good definition consists of the name for the general category to which something belongs (such as "war") followed by a list of every essential quality that belongs to anything within that category (in this case, being "hell"). Sometimes, a simple definition like that of Sherman can be effective in isolating a single, undeniable quality. Other times, one might look for a more comprehensive definition, such as the standard dictionary definition as "a state of open and declared, hostile armed conflict between states or nations." When seeking definitions, one should start with the dictionary. However, avoid citing the dictionary as an authority. One should look for more precise or poetic quotations from recognizable authorities that appeal to an audience's sensibilities. Whatever the definition one uses, the purpose of definition as a topic remains the same. It shifts attention from a close investigation into a particular thing to a more conceptual inquiry into the nature of that thing.

2   *Comparison.* **Comparison** takes two different things and puts them side by side to evaluate similarities and differences according to a common standard of value. Comparison asks the question "which aspects of one thing are superior or deficient compared to another thing?" The most important part of comparison, of course, is finding two things to

compare that have enough in common to be evaluated according to a common measure. For instance, Carl von Clausewitz famously argued that "war is not merely a political act, but also a real political instrument, a continuation of political commerce, a carrying out of the same by other means." By comparing the similarities between war and politics, Clausewitz sought to normalize war and make it a normal and acceptable means of attaining political goals. Sherman, by contrast, sought to compare war with hell in order to separate it from ordinary life because it values cruelty rather than civility. He argues that "war is cruelty, and you cannot refine it. Those who brought war into our country deserve all the curses and maledictions a people can pour out."

3   *Division.* To use the topic of **division** is to divide something that seems to be a "whole" into its component "parts" or combines disparate parts into a whole. Division that places the whole and the parts into some form of relationship to one another. The question of division is either "what parts constitute this thing?" or "what whole can these parts create?" Think of division like finding the ingredients to a recipe, mapping out a region, dissecting a body, building a block tower, or planning the steps of a vacation. Think of both what unites the parts in common purpose or function as well as what distinguishes each part from the other. One thing division helps you to do is focus on what relationship between parts, or between part and whole, is most important for your speech. A foreign policy, for instance, may involve diplomacy, economics, and policy. But if you follow Clausewitz, war that is most important is policy, for "war is part of policy, policy will determine its character. As policy becomes more ambitious and vigorous, so will war." Here is a relationship between a part (war) and a whole (policy). We do not need to include every part of something in our speech. Division is intended to help focus on which parts and relationships are important and those which are not.

4   *Cause and effect.* A relationship that two or more things in a functionally dependent relationship to one another in order to is to talk about **cause and effect**. This topic asks "how did this thing come about?" or "what does this thing cause to happen?" Unlike comparison, which simply shows how two things are similar or different, cause and effect asks how one thing influences another thing and brings about specific changes in that thing. For instance, the ancient Chinese general Sun Tzu once wrote that "the moral law causes the people to be in complete accord with their ruler, so that they will follow him regardless of their lives, undismayed by any danger." For him, seeking military victory requires the ruler to act in accordance with the moral law that gives an army its sense of virtuous purpose. Adherence to the moral law thus helps bring about honor in leadership and success in battle. As a topic of invention, cause and effect can often bring together things that might seem to be unlike each other on the surface but are linked

together through direct or indirect causes. For this topic, select any one of your resources, write it on a piece of paper, and start drawing potential causes and effects that can be traced back to this resource.

5   *Circumstance.* This topic considers what courses of actions or events are likely or unlikely to happen based on **circumstances**, which are the empirical contexts surrounding any particular action or event. Circumstance asks, "What actions are possible and impossible given the facts of the situation?" Another way of thinking about circumstance is to draw conclusions about future facts or events by referring to facts or events in the past. This topic overlaps with cause and effect, but is broader in scope. Sometimes past facts do not cause a future fact to come into existence, but act as more of a sign or indicator of something, just as good grades in high school makes it more possible that a student will go to college. The focus of circumstance is to determine whether or not someone should or should not do something (or, alternately, whether something can or cannot happen) in the future based on a careful reading of present contexts. To return to Sun Tzu, for instance, he once wrote: "If your enemy is secure at all points, be prepared for him. If he has superior strength, evade him. If your opponent is temperamental, seek to irritate him. Pretend to be weak, that he may grow arrogant." Each of these maxims point us to certain circumstances of the enemy and counsel possible actions to ward off attack and destabilize the enemy. That is, it is impossible to confront an enemy directly who has superior strength, but it is possible to irritate him when past facts have led him to be temperamental. When sketching out this topic, draw a solid line that represents two different outcomes, and list what are enabling or disabling factors that might decide each outcome.

To see how topics operate in a single speech, we might turn to one of the most fascinating orators in American history: civil rights champion and former slave Sojourner Truth. Born Isabella Van Wagenen (a Dutch name given by her Dutch slave owners) in about 1797, Truth achieved her freedom in 1827 and changed her name in 1843. Despite growing up illiterate, she was a woman of remarkable intelligence and presence. Her most famous extemporaneous address, "Ain't I a Woman?," was delivered at the Women's Convention in Akron, Ohio, on May 29, 1851. This type of convention was a major component of the early women's rights movement, which involved the organization of women's conferences to bring together feminists to discuss goals and strategies. However, many of these conferences attracted men (including several ministers) who came largely to heckle the speakers and to argue that women's proper place was one of being both subservient to and cared for by men. It was the heckling of one of these ministers that inspired Truth to speak. Reacting to a black-robed minister who argued for male superiority based on "superior intellect" and "manhood in Christ," Truth argued that women were in fact more powerful than men and also that black women had been denied even the limited rights given to white women. To make her case, she uses a variety of topics to challenge conventional understandings of race and gender:

> Well, children, where there is so much racket there must be something out of kilter. I think that 'twixt the negroes of the South and the women at the North, all talking about rights, the white men will be in a fix pretty soon. But what's all this here talking about?
>
> That man over there says that women need to be helped into carriages, and lifted over ditches, and to have the best place everywhere. Nobody ever helps me into carriages, or over mud-puddles, or gives me any best place! And ain't I a woman? Look at me! Look at my arm! I have plowed and planted, and gathered into barns, and no man could head me! And ain't I a woman? I could work as much and eat as much as a man— when I could get it—and bear the lash as well! And ain't I a woman? I have borne thirteen children, and seen most all sold off to slavery, and when I cried out with my mother's grief, none but Jesus heard me! And ain't I a woman?
>
> Then they talk about this thing in the head; what's this they call it? [member of audience whispers, "intellect"] That's it, honey. What's that got to do with women's rights or negroes' rights? If my cup won't hold but a pint, and yours holds a quart, wouldn't you be mean not to let me have my little half measure full?
>
> Then that little man in black there, he says women can't have as many rights as men, 'cause Christ wasn't a woman! Where did your Christ come from? Where did your Christ come from? From God and a woman! Man had nothing to do with Him.
>
> If the first woman God ever made was strong enough to turn the world upside down all alone, these women together ought to be able to turn it back, and get it right side up again! And now they are asking to do it, the men better let them.[5]

Truth's speech in many ways follows the precise order of the topics. First, she raises the question of **definition**: "What is a woman?" The definition given by the pastor was one of relative helplessness and dependency. Truth challenges this definition by asserting the strength and power of women, drawing her own personal narrative. Second, she **compares** the qualities of men and women and finds, through specific examples from her own life, that women share many qualities with men and in fact are superior in many ways. Third, she uses **division** to look at the different parts of women's lives, from bearing children, to plowing and planting, to eating and working, each part adding up to a complex whole. Fourth, she appeals to **cause**

5   Sojourner Truth, "Ain't I a Woman?" available at www.nps.gov/articles/sojourner-truth.htm (accessed March 24, 2022).

by drawing on the resources of myth asserting that the appearance of Christ on Earth was caused by the actions of a woman. Finally, she appeals to **circumstance** to show that it is impossible for men to suppress the power of women while claiming, again drawing on the Christian myth of Genesis, that it is possible for women to turn the world right side up again.

Stasis

Another method of invention is to interpret your subject matter as if it were occurring in a court trial and you were acting as either the prosecuting or defending attorney. In preparation for your speech in court, you would have to determine what were the established facts of the case and what aspects were in contention. In classical rhetoric, **stasis theory** is a tool to help decide what is at stake in an argument in order to focus attention on key points of conflict. The word "*stasis*" comes from the Greek word for "standstill" or "conflict," meaning the point at which two opposing forces have met and where the battle lines have been drawn. In rhetoric, points of stasis indicate the point in an argument that must be resolved in order for a discussion to come to a conclusion. There are five points of stasis: *fact, definition, quality, procedure*, and *policy*. As a method of invention, stasis demands that we ask four sets of questions about our subject to determine where the real conflict lies so we can focus our energies just as this point.

1   *Fact.* A **question of fact** asks: "Does something exist, has something happened, or has an effect been produced in a specific way that has a bearing on our decision?" A fact in stasis theory is not simply any point of data or information. It concerns the facts that are essential to know in making a judgment. In a court case, questions of fact are resolved in the stage of **discovery**, where both prosecution and defense admit their evidence so that both sides can see what will be presented as fact during the trial. Questions of fact involve the *who, what, when, where*, and *how* of a situation (the *why* is for another stasis point). They are akin to the forensic investigation of a crime scene that gathers available evidence and tries to reconstruct what occurred and who was present. For instance, questions of fact might involve, in current topics, whether or not the earth's climate is rising due to the burning of fossil fuels, whether Shakespeare was actually the author of *Hamlet*, whether humans evolved from earlier primates, whether the lost city of Atlantis actually exists, whether Lee Harvey Oswald shot John F. Kennedy, or whether a gluten-free diet is healthy.

2   *Definition.* A **question of definition** asks: "What's the best way to define this fact according to some established rule, meaning, or law?" Once we accept that a fact exists and plays a significant role in our decision-making process, the next step is to properly categorize this fact and place it within a wider context of meaning. Definition seeks to

"group" this fact by placing it within a category alongside other similar facts. Clearly, this point of stasis is very similar to the topic of definition. The only difference is that, being considered in the context of a debate, trial, or conflict, that one's choice of definition is specifically chosen to support or defend a person or idea. For instance, in a murder trial, one might decide a question of *fact* by identifying a bloody knife as the instrument for stabbing another individual. *Definition* would then classify the act as a "murder" and the knife as the "murder weapon" according to the law. The conflict arises when competing parties wish to define the same fact in different ways. If an individual took another person's bicycle to ride for a day, was this a "theft" or simply "borrowing"? In a political system where citizens can vote but the cost of campaigning means only the wealthy hold office, do we properly call this a "democracy" or an "oligarchy"? Definition looks for signs and evidence that a certain thing fits one category better than another.

3   *Quality*. A **question of quality** asks: "Given the fact and definition of a thing, should we evaluate its overall quality as good or bad, as frivolous, or important, as justifiable or worthy of condemnation?" Questions of quality accept that something exists and can be defined in a certain way; it places its emphasis instead on matters of value. By "quality," then, this stasis point refers to the property, tenor, nature, or character of something that transcends its mere existence. Often, questions of quality ask an audience to consider criteria that are outside the strict boundaries of definition and speak to broader social norms, values, and ideals. For instance, an individual who admits the fact of killing someone and thereby committing murder might argue, through quality, that the murder was justified through self-defense or for the greater good. John Wilkes Booth, for instance, after shooting Abraham Lincoln, shouted "*Sic semper tyrannis!*" (or "death to tyrants!") as a way of justifying the assassination. Conversely, one might reinterpret a seemingly honorable action, such as private philanthropy, as something worthy of blame if that charity was given only to bribe a population into voting them into office.

4   *Procedure*. A **question of procedure** asks: "Regardless of the fact, definition, or quality of something, is this the proper process or legitimate jurisdiction for judging this thing?" When emphasizing questions of procedure, speakers turn our attention away from the past facts of the case and toward the present circumstances in which the facts are being examined and judged. Questions of procedure call into question whether or not certain individuals and institutions have the right and authority to judge the case, as well as challenging (or defending) whether specific methods or procedures are the best fit for the character of the facts. In strictly legal contexts, for instance, questions of procedure determine whether a case will be tried in a local, state, federal, or international court. In politics, different parties might argue whether a

law is valid or invalid because of the process by which it was passed. Questions of procedure often have the result of "turning the tables" on the prosecution, making them defend the legitimacy of their position to pass judgment on the defendant, as when a rebellious child reaches the age when they feel that their parents have no right to judge or dictate their actions any further.

5   *Policy*. A **question of policy** asks: "Given the accepted facts, definitions, and qualities of the case, what type of actions, laws, rules, or strategies should be adopted in the future?" Policy thus overlaps with the deliberative genre of Aristotle that seeks to compare different courses of action based on expediency. In the case of a court trial, for instance, questions of policy might question whether the law that condemned or excused some action was, in fact, a just law. Asking whether the laws or policies should be altered in light of certain facts and events raises questions of policy. Often, the answer given to a question of policy grows out of answers to the previous questions. If, for instance, one rejects the facts of biological evolution in favor of divine creation, then policies that favor the teaching of evolution in schools should be changed. If gay couples are prevented from being married because of reliance of a definition as marriage as a union only between a man and a woman, then a speaker might recommend changing the definition of marriage. Any change in the structure of society to adapt to new conditions is a matter of policy.

Staying within the topic of women's rights, an example of the use of stasis theory in the case of a court of law can be found in the testimony of Susan B. Anthony. Anthony still appears on the face of some dollar coins, but it is not as well known that she also was convicted of a crime—the crime of casting a ballot in the 1872 presidential election, which happened during a time when women could not vote. On June 19, 1873, after having been denied the opportunity to say a word in her defense, she stood before Judge Ward Hunt after her lawyer appealed the guilty verdict. This excerpt from her interaction with the judge shows a defendant can make use of different aspects of stasis theory to refute accusations and challenge the authority of the court:

JUDGE HUNT: [Ordering the defendant to stand up] Has the prisoner anything to say why sentence shall not be pronounced?

MISS ANTHONY: Yes, your honor, I have many things to say; for in your ordered verdict of guilty, you have trampled underfoot every vital principle of our government. My natural rights, my civil rights, my political rights, my judicial rights, are all alike ignored. Robbed of the fundamental privilege of citizenship, I am degraded from the status of a citizen to that of a subject; and not only myself individually, but all of my sex, are, by your honor's verdict, doomed to political subjection under this, so-called, form of government.

JUDGE HUNT: The Court cannot listen to a rehearsal of arguments the prisoner's counsel has already consumed three hours in presenting.

MISS ANTHONY: May it please your honor, I am not arguing the question, but simply stating the reasons why sentence cannot, in justice, be pronounced against me. Your denial of my citizen's right to vote, is the denial of my right of consent as one of the governed, the denial of my right of representation as one of the taxed, the denial of my right to a trial by a jury of my peers as an offender against law, therefore, the denial of my sacred rights to life, liberty, property and ...

JUDGE HUNT: The Court cannot allow the prisoner to go on ... The Court must insist the prisoner has been tried according to the established forms of law.

MISS ANTHONY: Yes, your honor, but by forms of law all made by men, interpreted by men, administered by men, in favor of men, and against women; and hence, your honor's ordered verdict of guilty, against a United States citizen for the exercise of *"that citizen's right to vote,"* simply because that citizen was a woman and not a man. As then, the slaves who got their freedom must take it over, or under, or through the unjust forms of law, precisely so, now, must women, to get their right to a voice in this government, take it; and I have taken mine, and mean to take it at every possible opportunity.

JUDGE HUNT: The Court orders the prisoner to sit down. It will not allow another word... .[Here the prisoner sat down.]JUDGE HUNT: The prisoner will stand up. [Here Miss Anthony arose again.] The sentence of the Court is that you pay a fine of one hundred dollars and the costs of the prosecution.

MISS ANTHONY: May it please your honor, I shall never pay a dollar of your unjust penalty. All the stock in trade I possess is a $10,000 debt, incurred by publishing my paper—*The Revolution*—four years ago, the sole object of which was to educate all women to do precisely as I have done, rebel against your man-made, unjust, unconstitutional forms of law, that tax, fine, imprison and hang women, while they deny them the right of representation in the government; and I shall work on with might and main to pay every dollar of that honest debt, but not a penny shall go to this unjust claim. And I shall earnestly and persistently continue to urge all women to the practical recognition of the old revolutionary maxim, that "Resistance to tyranny is obedience to God."[6]

When defending herself, Anthony first admits the **fact** of the case that she voted in an election. Rather than trying to deny the act, Anthony embraces it. Second, Anthony insists on **defining** her action as an expression of her citizen's right to vote which conforms to a gender-neutral

6   Douglas O. Linder, "Susan Anthony Trial (1873)," available at https://famous-trials.com/Anthony (accessed June 6, 2022).

interpretation of the law. In applying this definition, she draws from specific social knowledge drawn from the principles of the founding of the nation. The judge, by contrast, asserts that he is upholding "established" forms of law and therefore applying conventional definitions based on clear gender distinctions. Third, Anthony professes that even if she violated the letter of the law, the **quality** of her action excuses the violation by reference to the myth of the American Revolution and its accompanying maxim, "resistance to tyranny is obedience to God." Fourth, she challenges the **procedure** of the court trial, denying the legitimacy of any law or process in which women are judged by rules developed and applied only by men. Lastly, she advocates a **policy** of overturning "man-made, unjust, unconstitutional forms of law" and implementing laws written in cooperation with women for the equal rights of all.

Conclusion

The methods of invention are tools for finding creative, credible, and striking content for your speeches. Each tool on its own may seem simple and direct. However, those two qualities are their power. Very often, we fail to see or even recognize resources that may be close at hand, simply because we have not turned our attention in that direction. Instead, we rely on the algorithms of digital search engines to do the work of invention for us, leading to speeches that lack personality, are very often wrong, and are almost always bland. The different methods of invention should thus be treated not individually but in relationship to the other parts. The most effective process of invention will employ each of its tools one at a time to find what is an available resource. Sometimes the methods of invention help us locate resources that we might already be carrying around inside of us, like maxims, narratives, and myths. Other times, they point us to look outside of ourselves into specific sources that require more careful research. But what is most impressive about these methods is how, by the end of our search, we often end up with an accumulation of resources that, taken together, are far more impressive than any one fact, example, or statistic on its own. The important thing in invention is to follow the method from beginning to end and not focus just on a few selected topics or resources. Invention requires patience. Creativity is as much a result of discipline as it is of inspiration.

Discussion Questions

1   Where, in your experience, do most young people get their news? Do you think they are more or less informed than the older generations?
2   How reliable is Wikipedia? Do you think these types of user-generated sources are an advance over traditional print resources?
3   How can you tell the difference between propaganda and legitimate news and facts?

4   Identify a recent controversy on social media about some transgression by a celebrity. Imagine this celebrity defending their actions through the different types of stasis.
5   Take a simple object, like a dog. What different aspects of a dog are emphasized when you examine it through definition, circumstance, division, comparison, and cause and effect?
6   When is a story more persuasive than a fact? By contrast, when would a story be out of place and considered a distraction?
7   How much of our everyday conversations and what degree of our practical judgments are determined by the informal and implicit resources of public memory?
8   In what types of public controversies is there a clear conflict between public memory and more specialized facts and statistics? How does this conflict play out rhetorically?

Exercises

1   **Defending maxims**: Choose a maxim that you remember a friend or family member using. Now write a short speech defending that maxim by using a fact, a narrative, an example, and testimony.
2   **Different topics**: Choose a subject that everyone in the class will use in their speech. Assign different topics to everyone in order to invent something to say. Write a brief speech that includes a thesis and three main points based on your topic.
3   **Court trial**: Split the class into 10 groups. Find a news article in print or on video about a specific trial that has attracted much public attention. Assign each group to defend or prosecute this person by assigning them one specific stasis point, definition, quality, procedure, fact, or policy, each side taking the opposite stance on each issue.

References

Consigny, Scott. "The Rhetorical Example," *Southern Speech Communication Journal* 41 (1976), 121–134.
Farrell, Thomas. "Knowledge, Consensus, and Rhetorical Theory," in *Contemporary Rhetorical Theory: A Reader*, ed. John Louis Lucaites, Celeste Michelle Condit, and Sally Caudill (New York: The Guilford Press, 1999).
Fisher, Walter. *Human Communication as Narration: Toward a Philosophy of Reason, Value, and Action* (Columbia, SC: University of South Carolina Press, 1987).
Fisher, Walter. "Narration as a Human Communication Paradigm: The Case of Public Moral Argument," in *Contemporary Rhetorical Theory: A Reader*, ed. John Louis Lucaites, Celeste Michelle Condit, and Sally Caudill (New York: The Guilford Press, 1999).
Linder, Douglas O. "Susan Anthony Trial (1873)," available at https://famous-trials.com/Anthony (accessed June 6, 2022).

Truth, Sojourner. "Ain't I a Woman?" available at www.nps.gov/articles/sojour ner-truth.htm (accessed March 24, 2022).

West, William. "Memory," in *Encyclopedia of Rhetoric*, ed. Thomas Sloan (Oxford: Oxford University Press, 2001).

5 Arrangement

Arrangement is the art of putting things together effectively. We make use of the skill of arrangement in many parts of our lives. We arrange the space of our bedrooms and our places of residence to make us feel comfortable. We arrange our desks and our offices to be more productive. We arrange the schedule of our day so we can balance work and leisure. We make arrangements to go out socially to enjoy each other's company. We arrange special dinners for family and friends during holidays and special events. In each case, we are arranging objects or time or people or events in a certain spatial and temporal order in order to bring about some desired effect. Similarly, we arrange how we express ourselves to others in words, actions, or images in order to communicate a desired meaning to other people and also to bring about certain experiences, feelings, ideas, or emotions. Public speaking is no different in this regard from any act of communication. It differs only in requiring a higher degree of arrangement in order to hold the attention of an audience and communicate meanings that are more complex or controversial than can be communicated in casual conversation or a social media posting.

If **invention**, or the discovery of something to say, helped gather a speech's **content**, or the specific arguments, stories, or facts that it contains, **arrangement** represents the step of giving order to a speech in anticipation of giving it "form." A form of a speech is not something intrinsic to a speech itself, as one might think of a shape of a container. Form is a product of the interaction between the speech and the audience and is found in the experience of the hearers of viewers. Following the ideas of Kenneth Burke, **form** is not an empty space waiting to be filled in with content, but rather an entire arc of temporal experience produced by symbols that first arouses the **appetites** of an audience, referring to the desires, curiosities, and interests that keep them listening, and then **satisfies** those appetites through a successful sequence of main points and a conclusion. **Monroe's motivated sequence**, for instance, is a good example of form by starting with need, moving through satisfaction, and ending in action. For Burke, therefore, not everything has form in this sense. Rather, a work has form insofar one part of the work arouses interest in what follows and then provides gratification. Similarly,

DOI: 10.4324/9781003316787-5

public speaking, too, requires a kind of *movement* from one place to another, a mental journey that begins at a familiar place and sojourns toward somewhere new. For instance, when Martin Luther King Jr. announces that he has a dream, makes us desire to observe the meaning of that dream, and then places that dream before us in a way that brings about feelings of hope, belonging, and unity—that is form.

From the earliest history of rhetoric, arrangement has been a crucial part of public speaking. For instance, in classical Roman oration, the arrangement was quite rigid and required a speaker to begin with an *introduction* (*exordium*) to state the speech's purpose and establish credibility, then proceed through a *statement of facts* (*narratio*) to provide an overview of the situation, *division* (*partitio*) to outline what is to follow and specify main point, *proof* (*confirmatio*) to present arguments and supporting facts, *refutation* (*refutatio*) to refute counterarguments, until ending up with the *conclusion* (*peroratio*), which summed up claims and reinforced them with emotional appeal. Any speaker who wished to have an influence in the political sphere of the Roman republic had to follow this arrangement or else violate the audience's expectations. Today we embrace a much looser and individualistic approach to arrangement. However, achieving form still requires following the proven techniques that can give an initial order to the chaos of material gathered together through invention. Nonetheless, the final arbiter of success is not how well the speech conforms to rigid rules and formulas; it is how effectively the arrangement captures the attention and interest of the audience and then moves them through the body of the speech until they reach a satisfying conclusion.

Specific Purpose

Public speaking is distinct from conversation or the more casual forms of mediated expression by being structured around a concrete goal called a **specific purpose** that is expressed as a specific argument or position to be explained and defended called a **thesis**. A specific purpose is the answer to the question, "How is this speech trying to influence an audience?" whereas a thesis is the answer to the question, "What is the claim being asserted or defended in this speech?" Especially for beginning speakers, the quality of a speech stands or falls with how well the thesis helps to achieve the specific purpose. The thesis is the center around which every aspect of a speech revolves. Conveying a thesis to the audience gives a speaker a concrete focus necessary to create a logical and coherent message and provides an audience reference point to understand the speech. Arrangement is grounded on having a specific purpose and a clear thesis.

A **specific purpose** is an expression of an interest in a particular goal that the speaker finds interesting and that may have value for an audience. It involves four characteristics: (1) the *genre of speech* one is giving; (2) the *audience* to which this speech is delivered; (3) the *occasion* for the speech; and

(4) the *effect* on the audience that the speech is supposed to have. Examples of specific purposes might include "to solicit (*genre*) my parents (*audience*) at a conversation over dinner (*occasion*) to buy me a car (*effect*)" or "to commemorate the Battle of Normandy during Memorial Day in front of a public audience to make them remember the sacrifices of veterans" or "to deliberate at the school board meeting in support of school uniforms." For a speech delivered in a public speaking class, the audience can either be the actual class or some imagined audience, depending on the decision of the instructor. In general, however, speeches given to actual audiences (that is, the class) generally have more value because one can gauge an actual rather than a hypothetical response.

A **thesis** is the specific argument that seeks to achieve the specific purpose. It is usually a single sentence that sums up what the entire speech is arguing, including a claim and reasons in support of that claim. Whereas a specific purpose is written for the speaker in order to help to *develop* a concrete idea during the writing process, a thesis is the *product* of that process. A thesis is an instrument to achieve a specific purpose. After studying the audience and its needs, beliefs, and desires, a speaker uses invention to gather resources related to the subject and constructs a thesis designed to provide clear reasons for adopting position, principle, policy, or idea. A thesis has three components: (1) a **topic** that defines your subject matter; (2) a **claim** that you are making about that topic; and (3) **reasons** why this claim should be adopted by the audience. Usually, the reasons for the claim are summaries of the three main points of a speech. For instance, at the school board meeting, one might say "school uniforms (*topic*) should be mandated for all students (*claim*) because they foster a sense of community, reduce bullying, and cut down on the clothing costs over time (*reasons*)." A thesis should always appear at the end of an introduction as a way of transitioning to a discussion of the main points. Let us imagine we are writing a thesis for the specific purpose "To persuade university students that they should support policies of a carbon neutral campus as a means to reduce greenhouse gasses and slow global warming." A thesis in support of the specific purpose should do the following things:

1   *Make a specific claim.* A thesis should be specific. Vague and generic thesis statements always lead to speeches that are vague, confused, and lacking in impact. The more specific you can make a thesis, the more focused your speech will become and the greater impact it will have on an audience. A thesis that relies on generalities like "we should tackle the problem of global warming" is less effective than one that tells us specifically "We must support a policy of a carbon neutral campus." A thesis should always seek to target a specific object, policy, or action that can be visualized more clearly than an abstract virtue or ideal. A thesis should help listeners visualize something clearly enough in their imagination that they can form a distinct judgment about it.

2 *Focus on a single topic.* Avoid including too many topics in a speech. An audience can only follow a few lines of reasoning in a sitting, and a speech that attempts to go too many places will lose them. Too many topics also generally lead to superficial arguments that do not get to the "heart" of an issue. With a public speech, do not try to do too much or you will not accomplish anything. For instance, there may be many issues and reasons to support a carbon neutral campus—economic, cultural, environmental, social, or ethical—but one should focus as much as possible on the topic that will make the most dramatic impact for those who are listening.

3 *Be audience centered.* Any topic should be developed only with respect to the situated interests of an audience. How do we know which topic to focus on? Think about what the immediate audience may be most concerned about. For instance, a speech on global warming addressed to the business community would obviously focus on the long-term economic benefits. A speech directed at a younger audience of university students, by contrast, might be more idealistic and focus on issues of quality of life in 50 years or the devastating effects it might have on coastal communities and underdeveloped countries. So a thesis might be expanded to say, "We university students have a responsibility to support a carbon neutral university campus in order to do our part to preserve our future."

4 *Present reasons/details.* Following the claim should either be *reasons* in support of the claim or *details* about how it will be elaborated. The claim "We should build this bridge ..." is generally followed by *reasons* like "because it will ease traffic, create a scenic walkway, and stop litter." But the claim "The universe is infinite ..." should be followed by *details* like "and I will show how it expands in all directions, has no center, and possesses infinite possibility." A thesis might also have some combination of both reasons and details. In our thesis about the climate accords, let us combine one detail and one reason: "As we witness dramatic increases in flooding, desertification, and devastating storms across the globe (*detail*), we university students (*audience*) have a responsibility to support a carbon neutral campus (*specific topic*) to reduce greenhouse gasses, demonstrate leadership as citizens, and experiment with new ways to cut emissions (*reasons*)." A thesis like this should be comprehensive enough that it can be quoted out of the context of the speech and yet still communicate its core message.

Introductions

Once you construct a specific purpose and thesis, it is time to build the speech. An **introduction** should arouse some desire or appetite in the audience to hear the remainder of the speech. An introduction is therefore a kind of promise. It tells the audience what they are going to hear and promises that if they stick around they will have an enriched experience. Introductions should thus be clear and interesting, ideally combining elements of argument and narrative that tell an audience that they will be hearing a well-informed argument as well as some interesting stories along the way. Broken down into specifics, the functions are as follows:

1   *Capture audience's attention.* Making an audience interested in listening to what you have to say is *the* most important function of an introduction. If they are not interested, then nothing else you say will matter because they won't hear it. The following are some helpful techniques to "get attention and interest" before stating your thesis and moving to the body. Let us continue using the example of global warming:

    a   *Use a quote.* Everyone enjoys hearing interesting quotes, regardless of whether they are from famous people or just one's grand-mother. Quotes should be relatively short and easy to understand, but also have a striking character that gives it the quality of a proverb or maxim. These quotes should then be relevant to your own topic and anticipate claims you might be making in your main points. For instance, one might catch attention to the problem of climate change by citing Pope Francis: "Ahead of his encyclical in 2015 he tweeted 'The Earth, our home, is beginning to look like an immense pile of filth.'" By placing these words in the mouth of Pope Francis, one imagines them coming out of his mouth and being delivered in person to the audience. Simply paraphrasing this quote will not do. One has to use the exact language that captures the personality of the speaker.

    b   *Present a startling fact.* Stating some dramatic fact either reveals some problem in graphic form (like the fact that thousands of people die from some disease every day) or it demonstrates the relevance of your topic (like the fact that the amount of candy eaten in a year, when stacked on a pile, would reach to some spectacular height). Speakers then proceed from this startling fact to argue the less exciting details that are necessary to understand and give meaning to that fact. For instance, "imagine, for a moment, standing on the coastline and looking out onto the Atlantic Ocean to see the sky-scrapers of Manhattan jutting out from the water." A startling fact should contain information that is significant as well as communicate that information through a clear and vivid image capable of being understood immediately. To be "startled" means that the fact must strike an audience in an instant without any further explanation.

    c   *Begin with a question.* To ask a question is to put your audience in the position of judgment. What would they do if such a thing occurred? What would they think about this or that idea? The intention of this strategy is to generate perplexity that your speech presumably would resolve. A poor question has an obvious answer, such as "If you had a choice, would you abolish cancer?" A good question raises some moral issue, such as "If your family was hungry, would you steal bread?" For instance, "Imagine if the cost of driving our cars or operating our air-conditioning could be paid in islands. Every year we would choose an island in the ocean, and it would disappear from the face of the earth. Would you pay that cost to keep cool?" A question should create a setting that poses a difficult choice. Questions should introduce the problem of the speech. Just make sure that you provide the resources to answer the question by the end.

d   *Refer to a current event.* Usually drawn from news stories, current events demonstrate why your topic is relevant to everyday contemporary life. These events may be *shocking* (like a child imitating violent video games in real life), *inspiring* (like a person who struggled to overcome cancer), or simply *odd* (like a man who thinks he is the king of Canada). In either case, they are used to show how violent video games, cancer cures, or psychological disorders, for example, are relevant issues to talk about. For instance, "In August of 2016, a rain storm struck southern Louisiana and dumped so much rain that it flooded virtually the entire city of Baton Rouge. They called it a 500-year storm, but in the last year it turns out that there were fifteen such 500-year storms across the United States." Clearly, this current event also communicates a startling fact, but it does so in the context of news. One might also end on a question.

e   *Tell a story.* A story in an introduction functions a lot like a fable. For instance, the "Boy Who Cried Wolf" conveys a lesson about trust. A story is a way of embodying some message by using plot and character as symbolic of a larger theme. Stories can come from personal experience, news, or history, or can be completely made up. However, completely fictional stories of the hypothetical variety are generally ineffective because the audience does not take them seriously. A good story relates some actual event, even if that event is your grandfather telling you a fictional story as a child. For instance, "In the Maldives islands, fisherman used to catch skipjack tuna with just a pole and line on the shore. But as the temperatures rise, the tuna are now swimming far offshore while the ocean itself is creeping up the beach and threatening to flood the coastal villages with every storm. The entire livelihood of the Maldives is now under threat." This story also is a type of current event, but it is told more as a narrative about a single individual that invites us to think of him as a protagonist in a drama.

f   *Perform a demonstration.* A technique with only very narrow applications, performing a demonstration involves actually doing some physical action to make a point. Anyone who has taken physics knows the typical kind of science demonstration meant to demonstrate how Newton's laws function. A demonstration can also be *entertaining* (like doing a magic trick), or *controversial* (like showing how a condom works). In either case, it catches attention through actions rather than just words. For instance, to show how melting ice caps can increase sea level, one might actually bring in a snowball and during the course of the speech have it slowly melt into a container and uncover a stone.

g   *Refer to literary material.* This strategy combines the strategy of quoting and telling a story. This is the one case in which fictional stories are effective because they derive from literature rather than just your imagination. The best source, of course, should be familiar to and appreciated by your audience, especially when it has acknowledged cultural significance for a larger community. For instance, one might quote a package from Moby Dick in which Herman Melville says it is impossible to imagine humans being able to ever threaten whales with extinction. This would show how important it is for us to come to terms with the damage humans can do to the environment.

h   *Use humor.* As anybody who has ever attended a religious service knows, humor is not always reserved for "light" topics. Humor can be effectively used in any situation. It takes a very sensitive touch to use humor when the "tone" of the speech is not a humorous one, but when done well it can be an effective way to "break the ice" with an audience. Humor might come in the form of a simple joke or pun or might be combined with telling a story or a current event. Humor is important because nothing increases our positive energy as much as laughing. For instance, one might start with the following joke: "Q: How many climate skeptics does it take to change a lightbulb? A: None. It's too early to say if the light bulb needs changing." This joke might come at the expense of the skeptics, but in a speech that encourages action, this sets the tone of what is to come.

i   *Create suspense.* Also a variation on telling a story, to create suspense you must set up conditions that may lead to some potential climax, thereby keeping your audience members on the edge of their seats. This suspense can be created through narrative or through demonstration. Effective suspense requires spending time setting the scene and then suggesting changes that might bring about an unexpected future, at each point giving the audience time to imagine what is to come. For instance, one might combine this with current events, telling a story, and asking a question. Even as simple as saying "Every year, the ocean creeps higher and higher along the East Coast. Just recently, we heard that another major glacier is breaking off an ice shelf. Let me ask you, when will New York City be underwater? Five years? Thirty years?" Suspense keeps the audience around to hear the answer to the question and hopefully hear a solution.

2   *State the topic and purpose of the speech.* Once you capture attention, you must retain it. An essential part of keeping attention is by making clear what your speech will be about so the audience will be prepared to sit through a more formal argument that may not be as "flashy" as your introduction. State your thesis as succinctly as you can, slowly but with deliberate emphasis. Although this may seem to be an overly dry and formal part of the introduction, in actual fact audiences enjoy being confronted with a clear claim that they are tasked with evaluating. Leaving your topic vague has the consequence of making your audience's mind wander to other topics.

3   *Relate the topic to your audience.* No topic is intrinsically interesting. Maintaining an audience's attention usually requires that they feel invested in what you have to say. Relating a topic to the interests and experiences of an audience creates this feeling of investment because what you say has value for *them*. Relating the topic to the audience should have already been incorporated to some degree in the thesis, but the introduction should make this connection stronger. For instance, "As university students, we often get wrapped up in our everyday concerns of going to classes and getting a job. But almost all of us dream of traveling to different locations, experiencing both nature and culture in new ways. Global warming threatens those dreams." Now that you have implicated global warming into their lives, they are apt to pay closer attention.

4   *Set a tone.* Letting an audience know whether you intend to be serious, ironic, funny, critical, or deferential is what it means to "set a tone." Doing so puts your audience in a frame of mind so that they know what to expect, just as audiences prepare themselves for a different "tone" at a comedy club than at a graduation ceremony or a funeral. For instance, with issues like global warming, one could set an apocalyptic tone that dwelled on the notion of threat, or one might establish a more optimistic tone that emphasizes the positive actions we can take together to remediate this threat. The problem remains the same, but it makes a big difference if we seek to scare an audience or make them enthusiastic. Setting a tone creates expectations that you can satisfy later in the speech.

5   *Preview main points.* Although not always necessary, laying out the basic sequence of arguments can be helpful, especially when making a fairly complex or lengthy speech. Previews are generally inappropriate for commemorative or introductory speeches because they are too formal, but advocacy or enrichment speeches generally benefit from laying out the order of points so that an audience knows what to expect. For instance, "Today I am going to first diagnose the global threat of global

warming to fragile ecosystems and communities, second show how the carbon neutral policies offer an incomplete but yet necessary step to address this problem, and third to discuss the ways in which we can support these accords both politically and in our everyday actions." Keep in mind that a preview of main points is different than stating the thesis. A thesis states what you are going to argue. A preview explains how you are going to make those arguments.

6   *Provide a transition to the body of the speech.* Always let your audiences know when the introduction is over and the actual body of the speech has begun. This encourages them to listen with a different set of expectations. Because they have committed themselves to listening to the speech, they no longer need speakers to "get their attention." They now want to hear the details. A transition lets them know when this shift has occurred. For instance, "Let me now turn to the crisis that we face as a global community." Transitions allow an audience to close the door on one topic and open the door onto another.

Body

If the primary function of the introduction is to arouse interest, the primary function of the body of the speech is to progressively move an audience toward satisfaction one step at a time. The **main points** are the most important claims made by the speech that are intended to support the main thesis. In fact, most of the time, the thesis itself indicates what the main points will be. Take, for example, our earlier thesis:

> As we witness dramatic increases in flooding, desertification, and devastating storms across the globe, we university students have a responsibility to support a carbon neutral campus to reduce greenhouse gasses, demonstrate leadership as citizens, and experiment with new ways to cut emissions.

The main purpose of the speech is to argue for the establishment of a carbon neutral campus. The main points are what are condensed into the three brief reasons given to support the main purpose. In the body of the speech, these brief reasons should be rephrased as complete sentences that are themselves concrete claims organized in a particular way. For instance, these three main points might be written out as follows:

1   First, previous experiments in reducing and recapturing carbon waste have shown carbon neutral policies both to be effective and cost-efficient in reducing greenhouse gasses.
2   Second, as university students being trained to be leaders for the coming generation, it is important that we set an example for others to follow in our own practices.

3   Third, because universities are the sites of cutting-edge technology and innovation, we should take advantage of the campus as a place of experimentation.

Main points can be thought of narratively like acts in a play or structurally like the rooms in a house. In both cases, each main point has its own separate purpose and character and yet only exists to support the construction of a whole work. Moreover, the house analogy should not be interpreted to mean that the rooms have only physical proximity to one another; a house is primarily made to live in, and rooms are constructed so that each room leads naturally to the next. A poor speech, like a badly designed house, will simply place things next to each other that shouldn't go together, like putting the main bathroom next to the kitchen and the dining room on the second floor. Likewise, a poor speech, like a badly written play, will introduce characters in the first act only to never mention them again and will jump from scene to scene without properly demonstrating their connection. In contrast, a good speech will feel like a guided house tour that reveals every aspect of the building's design and a dramatic three-act play in which all the major plot points are resolved in the final scenes. It will present the audience with a clear progression of ideas that they can easily follow so that they know what is coming. If a speech does not fit into any of these orders, then it is likely that the speech will be too disconnected to be effective.

When considering arrangement, one must therefore remember that not everything will fit into any one structure. A crowded speech lacks flow, unity, and order. Arrangement helps determine what resources gathered from invention will fit within the speech and what resources will be left behind. Each form of arrangement is thus fit only for one flow of argumentation and order and choosing a type of arrangement will also determine the very structure of the claims. When possible, fit the content to the demands of the arrangement, rather than the other way around. Let us see how a speech on global warming might adapt its main points for different types of arrangement. These are the basic ways of structuring main points, using as an example our global warming speech:

1   *Chronological.* Speeches that involve some process of time are suitable for chronological order that describes something from beginning to end. For example, chronological order is useful when doing *biographies* (the life of Martin Luther King Jr.), *events* (the development of the Industrial Revolution), or *processes* (how life may have developed on Mars). The essential character of chronological speeches is an emphasis on narrative storytelling, describing how events lead into one another and influence and are influenced by particular actors, whether they are individuals, groups, or nations. Think of chronological order as you would compose a three-act play, with each act shifting to a later scene in the drama. For instance, in an enrichment speech about global

warming, one might examine the early timeline of climate science using these three main points that show how our understanding of global warming developed over the centuries:

- Main point 1: "The Industrial Revolution began in 1760 and began the trend of increasing carbon dioxide in the atmosphere."
- Main point 2: "The first time a scientist described the atmosphere as a 'greenhouse' was in 1824, when Jean-Baptiste Joseph Fourier, a mathematician working for Napoleon, was the first to describe how Earth's atmosphere retains warmth on what would otherwise be a very cold planet."
- Main point 3: "The realization that human activity might alter the climate was in 1937, when British coal engineer George Callendar compiled all carbon dioxide measurements made over the previous 100 years and found that the amount of CO_2 was increasing."

2   *Spatial.* Whereas chronological order deals with differences across time, spatial order deals with differences across space. The classic geographical speech is a kind of "world tour" in which the speaker shows the different manifestations of something in different regions, whether the subject matter is language, culture, science, economics, history, war, or art. But space can also be used in a more general sense of describing anything diagrammatically, whether it is a microchip, the brain, a crime scene, a state capital, or the universe. What unifies a geographical orientation is how each "space" has a certain structure and quality that stand in relationship with other spaces so that they all add up to some sort of "whole," much as we might look at how individual states in the northeastern United States constitute a unity we call "New England." In the case of global warming, one might have the following structure that compares effects in three parts of the United States:

- Main point 1: "Disappearing glaciers, early snowmelt, and severe droughts will cause more dramatic water shortages and continue to increase the risk of wildfires in the American West."
- Main point 2: "Rising sea levels will lead to even more coastal flooding on the Eastern Seaboard, especially in Florida, and in other areas such as the Gulf of Mexico."
- Main point 3: "Forests, farms, and cities in the Midwest will face troublesome new pests, heat waves, heavy downpours, and increased flooding."

3   *Cause–effect.* The cause-and-effect order almost always deals with speeches concerned with informing an audience about factual knowledge needed to address some problem. Consequently, such speeches almost always deal with issues of process (like the ways COVID-19 is transmitted or how reduced tariffs increase international trade), because a process is something that causes change over time. What is important in

cause-effect speeches is clearly identifying and diagnosing the cause and then tracing very clear arrows to specific effects that are not attributable to other causes. Often these types of speeches are most important when the effects of something are unknown or the causes are contested. For example, claiming that "it is the dramatic increase in carbon dioxide emissions by human sources which have brought about the devastating effects of climate change" is necessary only to an audience who questions whether humans are, in fact, responsible. The following main points show a succession of causes, tracing the effects of burning fossil fuels to the impact on climate to the effects on culture:

- Main point 1: "Despite natural fluctuations in temperature, our current era of global warming is directly attributable to the human burning of fossil fuels such as coal, oil, gasoline, and natural gas, which results in the greenhouse effect."
- Main point 2: "Scientists agree that the earth's rising temperatures are fueling longer and hotter heat waves, more frequent droughts, heavier rainfall, and more powerful hurricanes."
- Main point 3: "With the loss of farmland and increase in costs, instability in the international food markets could spark famines, food riots, political instability and civil unrest worldwide."

4   *Problem–solution.* This speech lays out the problem and then addresses that problem by presenting a clear solution. It typically integrates a cause-effect argument as the first and sometimes second main points, with the last point reserved for the satisfying solution. For instance, Monroe's motivated sequence follows the problem-solution order. These types of orders are best for solicitation, advocacy, and deliberation speeches that seek to focus the audience on a single policy or action that can respond to a particularly pressing issue. What is important in this arrangement is to only define those problems that the solution can address. Sometimes problems have many different aspects, and a speaker can get carried away listing each of them. However, a speech is only effective to the degree that the proposed solution can address every problem that is identified, no more and no less. In a speech on carbon neutrality policies at a university, one would begin with a specific challenge that could be met with these solutions:

- Main point 1: "Concerns about the increasing pace and intensity of global climate change and the potential for unprecedented harmful effects on our world have put pressure on institutions of higher education to demonstrate leadership if they are to keep pace with innovation."
- Main point 2: "Implementing policies leading to a carbon neutral campus is now possible by an investment in renewable energy that offsets any greenhouse gas emissions it produces."

- Main point 3: "Being at the forefront of these policies, universities benefit from demonstrating leadership and innovation in addressing the serious social, economic, and environmental issues associated with global warming in addition to the practical benefits of making changes before they become mandated by law."

5   *Pro–con.* The pro–con order is the counterpart of the cause–effect order in that it deals with the analysis of solutions that respond to problems. A pro–con order examines a particular solution to a problem and articulates its positive and negative qualities in order to provide an audience with sufficient objective knowledge to make a decision. For instance, even a simple decision of where to go out to dinner may result in a pro-con structure, with the menus and atmosphere of each restaurant being compared and contracted. A version of the pro-con order is the *comparative advantage* order, which in effect simply looks at comparative "pros" while leaving aside the drawbacks. Both of these arrangements rely on embedding causal arguments and narratives within at least two columns, side by side. In a three-part speech, typically the first two points offer the comparison with the third point advocating a choice. A speech that compares two options for reducing carbon emissions may look like this:

- Main point 1: "One technological solution focuses on development of carbon neutral technologies relying on renewable energy, like windmills, solar farms, and electric cars, that can significantly reduce emissions, even as they do not actually reduce carbon levels already in place."
- Main point 2: "Another strategy seeks to actually pull carbon from the atmosphere, including spraying aerosols of sulfate particles into the stratosphere or developing carbon capture technologies, which have the benefit of reducing levels but at the risk of potentially disrupting climate in unexpected ways."
- Main point 3: "Given the fact that geoengineering may have unexpectedly disastrous impacts, the current pursuit of carbon neutral technology in the near future is the surest way to combat global warming, although geoengineering must continue to be developed to confront the worst case scenario."

6   *Topical.* Perhaps the most frequent arrangement structure for speeches of enrichment and commemoration is topical, which means a series of related qualities or characteristics of your subject matter. These topics are not related by time, cause, effect, advantage, or comparison. Rather, they represent different qualities inherent in the subject matter itself that can be discerned by breaking the whole into parts, much like the topic of division. Examples might be "The four unique aspects of Louisiana cooking," "The hierarchies of English feudalism," and "Varieties of world religions." A topical order can be thought of as a kind of prism by

which we analyze a single topic (the "white light") by separating it into its different qualities (the different "color spectrums"). The idea is that by looking at each specific aspect of a topic, we will then be able to put it back together to create a sense of a whole. For instance, "There are three essential parts of good study habits, including a quiet space, regular habits, and a time when you are most awake." Think about topical order as a thorough description of something, taking each part at a time to describe in detail before moving to the next. For instance, a speech might look at the different types of geoengineering to remove carbon from the atmosphere.

- Main point 1: "One of the theories proposed for reducing global warming involves deflecting heat away from the Earth's surface with solar shields or satellites with movable reflectors."
- Main point 2: "Another technological fix involves 'sequestration,' the storage of CO_2 either deep underground or deep in the ocean."
- Main point 3: "Lastly, 'ocean fertilization,' entails scattering iron powder throughout the world's seas, providing nutrients to boost the amount of phytoplankton that thrive in the water's upper layers."

7   *Logical.* Although often included under the "topical" order, it is useful to think of logical order as a separate category. Whereas topical ordering focuses on the parts of a whole, logical reasoning is more analogous to mathematical reasoning that lays out evidence, premises, and conclusions in a clear sequence. Logical ordering arranges main points according to a structured movement of ideas that either moves from particular evidence to general conclusion (what we call **inductive reasoning**) or from general principle to specific application (what we call **deductive reasoning**). For instance, an inductive main point might be "the prevalence of fast-food restaurants on virtually every major intersection of every American town and city is an indicator of how much the American diet has come to rely on fast food." An example of deductive reasoning might be "Because frying oils and animal fats all are high in cholesterol, the foods most popular in fast food restaurants lead to a high cholesterol diet." What is important in logical ordering is that a speaker tries to move an audience from point A to point E by following the path through main points B, C, and D, with each main point building upon the conclusions of the previous main point, thus providing the speech with a kind of logical momentum. For instance, the first thesis you saw at the beginning of this section followed a logical order, starting first with an inductive argument that justified adopting carbon neutral policies, followed by two deductive arguments about the ethical responsibility of students and the innovative character of universities:

- First, previous experiments in reducing and recapturing carbon waste have shown carbon neutral policies both to be effective and cost-efficient in reducing greenhouse gasses.
- Second, as university students are being trained to be leaders for the coming generation, it is important that we set an example for others to follow in our own practices.
- Third, because universities are the sites of cutting-edge technology and innovation, we should take advantage of the campus as a place of experimentation.

As stated earlier, these methods of arrangement should be thought of as different ways of putting the same material together to produce different effects. Although there are exceptions, for the most part almost any general topic can be arranged using any of these methods. Sometimes, to get started, you should think only in very general terms rather than sketch out each set of main points. By comparing and contrasting different forms of arrangement, you might land upon an approach that seems unique and interesting. For instance, let us say you are interested in giving an enrichment speech about Martin Luther King Jr.'s civil rights rhetoric. By examining the topic through each of these lenses of arrangement, a speaker can experiment with different ways of presenting the speech.

1   *Chronological*: How King's oratory changed over time.
2   *Spatial*: Speeches given in the rural South versus the urban North.
3   *Cause–effect*: The impacts that his speeches had on civil rights legislation.
4   *Problem–solution*: How methods of nonviolence can also meet today's challenges.
5   *Pro–con*: The benefits and drawbacks of using nonviolent resistance methods.
6   *Topical*: Racism, poverty, and war as three major themes in his speeches.
7   *Logical*: The principles that justified breaking unjust laws.

Testing out these different perspectives can be very useful in generating new ideas on a topic that may not have been obvious to a speaker at first. They force us to look at a familiar object in different ways and therefore make us ask new questions to arouse new interests.

Transitions

Once you have sufficiently articulated a main point and concluded a section, it is necessary to provide a "bridge" to move your audience from one idea to another. A transition provides this bridge by showing the connection between the two ideas and the need to proceed from one to the other. For example, imagine two main points of an enrichment speech about the need for a carbon neutral campus. A transition between the last two main points of the logical arrangement might be: "And what applies to university students also goes for the universities themselves; each must take the lead in their respective spheres." This passage shifts our attention from one object (students) to another (universities) that are nonetheless connected by the idea that they both take on the burden of ethical responsibility. Here is a list of possible transition phrases:

1   Transitions between similar points:

- In the same way ...
- Likewise ...
- Equally ...
- This is similar to ...
- Similarly ...

2   Transitions between disagreeing points:

- Conversely ...
- Despite this ...
- However ...
- On the contrary ...
- Now let's consider ...
- Even so ...
- Nonetheless ...
- We can't ignore ...
- On the other hand ...

3   Transition to a significant issue:

- Fundamentally ...
- A major issue is ...
- The crux of the matter ...
- A significant concern is ...

Internal Previews

An internal preview is a sentence within the speech that lets an audience know what they are about to hear. For example, "In describing the ethical responsibility that university students have to confront global warming, I will tell three different stories of three different students, each working in their own way to contribute to a solution." Previews of this kind are helpful with a long speech that contains complex details. For shorter, less complex speeches, internal previews are often unnecessary. Phrases to use in internal previews might be "In my next points, I shall ..." or "The evidence that follows will show ..." or "Keep in mind that the main argument is ..." A preview establishes clearly what idea should be at the forefront of an audience's mind as they consider the details of each main point.

Internal Summaries

An internal summary reminds an audience of the key takeaway of the preceding argument, thereby reaffirming some important point that is important to keep in mind as the speech develops. For example, at the end of the first main point you could write, "In summary, carbon capture is neither fantasy nor futility; it is a practical and effective policy for both economic savings and greenhouse gas reduction." A summary should restate the idea of the main point but do so in a way that refers to the specific forms of evidence presented in the section. Examples of internal summaries include statements like "I have reviewed ...," or "Now that I have talked about a couple of the key points ...," or "to summarize briefly what was just discussed ..."

Signposts

A signpost is a way of saying to your audience "You are here." It marks a path along the way and lets them know your location. In the earlier articulation of the main points, these took the form of "First," "Second," and "Third." Other signposts include "To begin," "In conclusion," "Next," "Finally," and so forth. These very simple tools make a big difference in the way an audience follows along. It not only lets them count each main point and distinguish it from minor points and evidence, but it also lets them anticipate the end of the speech when it arrives. Signposts are ways of keeping time, as it were, which reduces the uncertainty and anxiety of an audience.

Conclusions

Whereas the purpose of the introduction is to get attention and interest, the purpose of the **conclusion** is to satisfy an audience's desires and make them feel as if the speech has come together as a whole and therefore achieved qualitative unity in form. Specifically, the conclusion should always perform two essential functions irrespective of persuasive strategy. First, it should *help the audience remember the speech*. Audiences need to be left with something concrete in their imagination that helps them recall what was said. Sometimes this can be achieved by calling attention to the physical environment so that your speech is linked to some memorable object or event that is present. Other times you recall something important or imaginative in the earlier part of the speech and emphasize it again so as to leave the audience with a lasting "impression." Second, it should *clearly end your speech*. Let people know when you are nearing the end of your speech. Letting an audience know that you are about to end gives them a sense of "closure" and encourages concentration and attention even if they might have drifted off during the body. Otherwise, a conclusion can end with a variety of different strategies:

1 *Leave with a call to action.* Persuasion sometimes requires a lengthy detour through factual accounts, narratives, reasons, and explanations. A conclusion should show how all of these things lead to a specific action that is within reach of the audience. This helps it end on *a positive note.* Even with speeches that articulate the most graphic and devastating conditions, audiences want to know that there is some hope in making the world a better place. It is important to give audiences this hope at the end of a speech so that they leave believing they can make some small difference. For example, "We can meet this challenge of global warming! But first we must convince those around us that it is a serious problem. Talk to someone close to you today to start changing minds one at a time." A call to action leaves the audience feeling potentially empowered.

2 *Startle your audience.* After a long speech, sometimes audiences get too relaxed or even bored. A conclusion that makes some startling claim or demonstration can "wake them up" and make them pay closer attention to your concluding arguments. For example, "Look out the window at campus and imagine that all you see is water. That is the fate that is faced by millions of people today in island and coastal communities."

3 *Challenge your audience.* Similar to startling the audience, a speaker can also take the risky move to challenge them. This usually involves a combination of critique and imagination. To challenge an audience means to suggest that they are not living up to their potential, and that a better future may be ahead of them if they rise to new heights. For example, "We all might care about this global problem, but we will soon be absorbed in our own daily routines. Take a moment every day to step out of those routines and change one habit, however small, in your life if only to remind yourself of the collective habits we must change as a nation."

4 *Come full circle.* A very effective way of concluding a speech is to refer to the introduction and pick up where it left off. If it asked a question, then answer it. If it began with a story, give that story an ending. If it quoted a famous philosopher, quote that philosopher again. This does not mean simply repeating what is already said but continuing a line of thought and bringing it to a proper conclusion. For example, "In 50 years, the grandchildren of the fishermen in the Maldives will have been born. Let us all work so that they might fish on those same shores rather than having them exist only in a faded photograph or memories."

5 *Visualize a positive future.* One way of ending on a positive note is to dramatize the great future that will come about through the committed actions of the audience. This is the basic strategy of much advertising that features before-and-after sequences. Thus, you not only want to tell people that their future is going to be better; you want to visualize that future for them in order to develop an emotional attachment. For instance, "If we only have the commitment, in only a few decades we can have virtually every automobile produced in the country run on

electric energy. We can invest in technology to remove carbon dioxide from the atmosphere. We can restore the coastlines which have already been eroded. This we can do together."

6   *Visualize a negative future.* The opposite strategy is to visualize the negative future that would come about from inaction or choosing a different action. In the advertising analogy, this would be the future of choosing the competitor's product. Instead of a popular person wearing a colorful line of new clothes, for example, one would show a sad and lonely person wearing his or her old wardrobe. For instance, "If we do nothing, millions of people will be condemned to living in squalid refugee camps. All of our great coastal cities will be underwater. And the cultural richness which has grown up over millennia in harmony with the environment will be lost."

7   *Ask a question.* Unlike the introduction, which poses a question that will then be answered, this question should leave the audience with something to ponder. For instance, "Will you do nothing?"

8   *Use quotations.* This strategy is identical to using a quotation in an introduction, except that the quotation should sum up the points that have come before and leave us with some kind of eloquent maxim to remember. For instance, one might quote Henry David Thoreau on the importance of nature to civilization or quote Genesis on how humans were commanded to tend the garden.

9   *Tell a story.* Often used effectively to give "moral lessons," a story at the conclusion of a speech sums up in narrative what was already explained using logic. A story can also be used simply to encourage the audience to laugh or to cry or to feel some kind of emotional response. For instance, returning to another story about an island community to generate concern, or telling a satirical story of a climate change denier to generate laughter.

Spoken Citation Style

As you fill the body of your speech with sources to justify your main points, it is important to know how to properly cite sources. This gives a speech credibility by demonstrating that the facts are not just your opinions but come from established and trusted sources. However, citing sources should not be overly technical, but just long enough to fit fluidly within a speech. Here are some guidelines for how to smoothly incorporate citations into your speech.

1   *Well-known and uncontroversial facts.* There is no citation needed for the obvious. Do not clutter a speech by citing things an audience takes for granted.

   • GOOD: "Over 2,000,000 people were killed in the Civil War."
   • BAD: "According to *Encyclopedia Online* ..."

2 *Unknown or controversial facts released by people and institutions in press releases.* When your information comes directly from the source and you have access to that source, just cite that original source by name. Do not cite any subsequent news publication that may have repeated this information.

- GOOD: "The Economy Institute released a report in June that claimed environmental restrictions hurt economic growth."
- BAD: "*The Times* reported in July that a report by the Brookings Institute in June said ..."

3 *Unknown or controversial facts published secondhand by news publications.* When a newspaper has cited some startling fact, make sure to cite *both* the source and the news publication that first reported it. The fact is that sometimes news reports will "spin" facts in certain ways, so it is important to acknowledge that you are getting it secondhand.

- GOOD: "Hodgedale Industries recently was reported in the *New York Times* as saying that its medical screening technologies have saved over 2,000 women's lives in the year 2001."
- BAD: "*The New York Times* claims that Hodgedale Industries has saved ..."
- BAD: "Hodgedale Industries has saved ..."
- BAD: "Hodgedale Industries claims to have saved ..."

4 *Quoting famous people.* Generally, important quotes by famous people only need a citation by the name of the person, not the time, place, or manner in which the passage was written or spoken.

- GOOD: "Socrates once said that 'the unexamined life is not worth living.'"
- BAD: "In 430 BC, Socrates was once quoted in Plato's *Critias* that ..."

5 *Quoting professionals or experts.* For all other quotes, cite the name, status or position, and the forum in which the quote appeared.

- GOOD: "In the *New York Times*, of Sept. 3, Gail Hansen, an epidemiologist who works for Pew Charitable Trusts, said 'at some point the available science can be used in making policy decisions.'"
- GOOD: "In today's *New York Times*, a notable epidemiologist said ..."
- BAD: "Gail Hansen said ..."
- BAD: "The *New York Times* reported that 'at some point ...'"

6 *Citing bare, uncontroversial facts reported in newspapers.* For isolated facts that do not merit a lot of attention, just cite the publication in which that fact appeared.

- GOOD: "The *New York Times* reported in 2010 that 34 percent of the population is obese."
- BAD: "Thirty-four percent of the population is obese."
- BAD: "A study based on national surveys that record heights and weights of a representative sample of Americans, in which people are considered obese if their body mass index—a ratio of height to weight—is thirty or greater, noted that 34 percent of the population is obese."

7 *Using stories or anecdotes found in magazines or websites.* When you use examples, it is important to make them sound like stories. The temptation is to ignore the need for citation. However, it is very important to cite the source and its author to give examples credibility. You simply need to find a discrete way to fit it in without ruining the flow of the narrative.

- GOOD: "Anna had just arrived from Russia when she was arrested by police, who accused her of spying. She was put in a cell for two months and was not able to see anyone. Her story, finally told last August in *The New Republic*, raises serious questions about our civil liberties."
- BAD: "Anna had just arrived from Russia when she was arrested by police, who accused her of spying. She was put in a cell for two months and was not able to see anyone. Can we let this happen in the United States?"
- BAD: "In a recent issue of *The New Republic*, a story appeared about a girl …"

Outlining

The final product of effective arrangement is the outline, which is the primary tool for helping to arrange all of your "discoveries" into a concrete form. **Outlining** allows you to organize the "highlights" of a speech into sections and put them into a linear progression of beginning, middle, and end. A **tentative outline** is an early, rough plan for the speech that allows a speaker to experiment with different arrangements before exerting the time and energy required to finalize the speech. In a classroom setting, a working outline also provides a medium of communication between instructor and student during the composition process. As a collaborative medium, outlines are often more valuable when they are incomplete, because they help identify the gaps that need to be filled. In the *creative stage*, a tentative outline should function as both a rough draft and a brainstorming session. The rough draft aspect records the basic arguments, facts, quotes, and strategies that the writer confidently feels are useful. The brainstorming aspect puts them together with ideas and possibilities that may not yet have any clear structure or backing. Both students and instructors should thus use outlines *as a tool for collaborative communication* during the process of invention and development. The **final outline** then represents the last stage of your speech preparations that precede the actual writing or delivery of a speech and is useful both for evaluation purposes (for the instructor) and to allow the speech to be performed again (for the speaker). The author should be careful to accurately record all quotations in full, as well as dutifully record all facts as faithfully as possible.

To be effective as a tool for creative composition, an outline should identify not only the content of what is going to be said but also the composition methods being used to organize the material. This includes not only methods outlined in this chapter but also the more specific strategies in subsequent chapters. Each specific entry should therefore include not only examples, arguments, and proofs, but also labels (in parentheses) attached to those examples, arguments, and proofs that tell both the student and the speaker what persuasive strategy is being employed. The outline should also include a bibliography with sources cited according to MLA style (or the instructor's preferred style) discussed in the previous section on invention.

When adding elements to your outline, you should follow a few general rules to determine what to include and how much to write. What is important is that you do not simply write out a full transcript of your speech and then simply break them into numbered sections. An outline is not a manuscript. It is a condemned summary of your argument that provides a loose framework on which you can construct a speech without being overly scripted.

1   Write out the **specific purpose** and **thesis** exactly as described in their respective sections.
2   Any **quotations,** including **maxims,** should be included in full and in quotation marks, with proper citation form that refers to a reference in the works cited.
3   **Main points** and **transitions** should be written out exactly as they will be spoken.
4   However, all other resources used in the sub-points, for instance, **narratives, examples, facts, myths**, or **statistics**, should only be briefly summarized and include only the essential parts and just enough to indicate what should be said. Write them as if you are telling someone what you are "going to say," rather than what you will literally say. For instance, "Narrative of going fishing with my dad as a kid, he used to tell me a myth of the day he caught the Big One" or "World Health Organization statistic, 10 million cancer deaths in 2020." Except for lengthy quotations, any entry should be no longer than two lines long, and often are only one line.
5   Make sure you label the tactics, forms, orders, resources, and any other aspect that describes any specific entry according to the book's terminology. Add these in italics within parentheses at the beginning of each entry. Sometimes an entry might have many different tactics used at the same time, for instance (*narrative, startling fact*).

An outline should follow this general template:

Title:

Specific purpose:

Introduction: *(introduction tactics)*

Transition:

Thesis:

Transition:

Body *(Type of arrangement order)*

1   **First main point**: *(type of argument)*

   a   **Subpoint 1**: *(tactic)*
   b   **Subpoint 2**: *(tactic)*
   c   **Subpoint 3**: *(tactic)*

Transition:

2   **Second main point**: *(type of argument)*

   a   **Subpoint 1**: *(tactic)*
   b   **Subpoint 2**: *(tactic)*
   c   **Subpoint 3**: *(tactic)*

Transition:

3   **Third main point**: *(type of argument)*

   a   **Subpoint 1**: *(tactic)*
   b   **Subpoint 2**: *(tactic)*
   c   **Subpoint 3**: *(tactic)*

Conclusion: *(conclusion tactic)*

Works cited

Sample Outline 1

Title: College Safety

Specific purpose: To explain how to get to and in your apartment in a safe way.

Introduction: *(Startling fact and begin with a question; ethos; exigence)* Have you ever been walking to the door of your college apartment and gotten the spooky feeling that something is wrong? College assaults and break-ins happen more often than you think. According to a 2019 study by the

Department of Justice, college aged individuals (18–24) are most likely age group to be victims of crime.

Transition: *(Evoked audience)* I know as college students with busy lives and schedules, the safety of you and your crowded college apartment can often slip your mind.

Thesis: Remaining safe and diligent when traveling to, entering, and living in your college apartment is a necessary and often neglected measure.

Transition/preview: First, I will talk about some methods to ensure that your journey home to your apartment is safe.

Body *(Chronological)*

1   **First main point**: *(Principle)* It is just as important to be careful when traveling as it is to be safe when you arrive.

    a   **Subpoint 1**: *(Example)* Be aware of surrounding cars, check backseat before getting in the vehicle. Example of woman who had a guy in her backseat after gas station trip.

    b   **Subpoint 2**: *(Cause)* Lock doors as soon as you get in, watch for following cars as you drive. Even when in a rush, it doesn't take long to glance in back seat and be aware of surroundings.

Transition: Now that you've effectively driven to your apartment, the next step is to take the long journey from the lot to your door.

1   **Second main point**: *(Causal)* Especially at night, coming home to a dark parking lot and having to walk through your building alone can be risky.

    a   **Subpoint 1**: *(Style)* Try and park near a light source. Walk quickly with no distractions to your door.

    b   **Subpoint 2**: *(Metaphor, maxim)* carry weapon? don't have to be a soldier armed to the teeth, but a weapon can help. If you have a weapon, that is a huge deterrent to criminals. The best form of defense is attack.

Transition: Okay, so you finally made it inside your apartment. Doing a couple of checks to make sure that your house is secure is the final act before you can relax and go about your day.

1   **Third main point**: *(Causal)* It is imperative that you secure your home before you go about your day.

    a   **Subpoint 1**: *(Example, distinction)* Lock your door. Example of my break-in.

    b   **Subpoint 2**: *(Style, contingency)* Be generally observant to see if anything is out of place.

Conclusion: *(Call to action, positive note)* You can never be 100% diligent or 100% safe. But by adding a few steps to your daily routine, you can significantly minimize the risk of getting hurt or stolen from. We can meet these challenges and make our community safer for all.

Works cited

1. Hustmyre, Chuck, and Jay Dixit. "How to Avoid Being a Victim." *Psychology Today*, Jan. 1, 2009. www.psychologytoday.com/us/arti cles/200901/how-avoid-being-victim.
2. Morgan, Rachel E, and Jennifer L Truman. "Criminal Victimization, 2019." *U.S. Department of Justice Bureau of Justice Statistics*, Sept. 2020. https://bjs.ojp.gov/content/pub/pdf/cv19.pdf
3. Singer, Samantha. "Life Saving Advice after Nashville Woman Escapes Suspect Hiding in Her Backseat." *FOX 17*, May 22, 2018. https://fox17.com/news/local/life-saving-advice-after-nashville-woman-escap es-suspect-hiding-in-her-backseat. Accessed Oct. 13, 2021.

Sample Outline 2

Title: Sex Education, The Topic which Shall Not Be Named

Specific purpose: advocate for better sex education policies in Texas to fellow A&M students

Arrangement: Logical

Introduction: *(refer to current situation, ask a question, personal narrative, definition)* How many of you went to school here and received proper sex education? Texas ranks very low in states providing sex education because the current law does not require it. I want to make sure our younger siblings, cousins, or even generations will gain the knowledge that is necessary in our lives.

Thesis: Texas should have higher regulations regarding sex education in schools because it will directly result in healthier outcomes, safer choices, greater morale.

Preview: Personally, I have never received any information regarding Sex Ed. My version of learning consists of reading the news about harassment cases or getting my first period totally unprepared.

Transition: Now let's talk about the reasons why Texas schools should require a sex education course. Not only will it directly help children have healthier outcomes, but it will ensure safer choices, and increase overall morale.

Body *(Logical order)*

1   **First main point**: *(Generalization)* California laws set an example for the nation, and if applied, Texas will also experience the same positive outcomes as California.

   a   **Subpoint 1**: *(Stats)* Texas ranks as one of the states to offer the lowest amount of sex education (little to none).

   b   **Subpoint 2**: *(Example)* California law requires school districts to provide comprehensive sex education (3 pieces of legislation that targeted all aspects of sex education).

Transition: Now that we can confirm that Texas would benefit from adopted policies like California, let's talk about how we know that sex education works to make safer choices.

1   **Second main point**: *(Sign)* Consistently making safer choices about sexual practices is an indication of having been properly educated.

   a   **Subpoint 1**: *(Statistic)* According to the CDC, Texas right now is ranked 5th highest state with teen births. Part of that reason is the lack of proper sex education.

   b   **Subpoint 2**: *(Narrative)* When you see people making those safe decisions like using a condom, or taking birth control, immediately you can infer that they have received proper sex education and are making those safe choices because of it. Wouldn't you want that too?

Transition: Now that we have identified what it takes to make such safer choices, let's talk about personal effect it has on you.

1   **Third main point**: *(Cause)* Sex education will lead to an increase in personal morale and understanding.

   a   **Subpoint 1**: *(Example)* Teaching them about genders and sexual orientation at an early age …

   b   **Subpoint 2**: *(Cause)* … leads them to expand their vocabulary from narrow to mindfulness and increase their empathy.

Conclusion: *(Visualize negative future, metaphor)* Currently Texas is facing the opposite effect. Teen pregnancies increasing, harassment cases increasing, discrimination increasing. In a nation that is so technologically advancing, we are lacking socially. Giving Texas the choice between teaching sex education or not is not working, we need a mandate to require sex education in schools.

Works cited

1. "Texas State Profile." *SIECUS*, Sept. 27, 2021. https://siecus.org/sta te_profile/texas-fy21- state-profile/
2. "California State Profile." *SIECUS*, Sept. 28, 2021. https://siecus. org/state_profile/california-fy21-state-profile/
3. Swaby, Aliyya. "Texas Education Board Approves New Sex Ed Policy That Does Not Cover LGBTQ Students or Consent." *The Texas Tribune*, Nov. 19, 2020, www.texastribune.org/2020/11/18/ Texas-sex-education-LGBTQ/.
4. Tfn. "5 Takeaways from the Texas Sex Ed Debate." *Texas Freedom Network*, Dec. 3, 2020, https://tfn.org/5-takeaways-from-the-texa s-sex-ed-debate/.

Notecards

Notecards are used for extemporaneous speaking as a means of reminding the speaker of the order and content of material to be presented. Although based on the substance of the outline, they should not simply consist of the entire outline cut into small pieces of paper. Notecards act primarily as reminders rather than a manuscript. Only quotes, transitions, theses, and introductory and concluding remarks can be written out, although speakers should strive to reduce even this material to a minimum. Although it is tempting to add more "just in case," the fact is that the more one writes on a notecard, the more a speaker is tempted simply to read out loud, thereby ruining the purpose of extemporaneous speaking. Notecards should not be too "packed" with information, but should be written in clear, bold letters with a lot of "white space" so that one can easily see what comes next without having to hunt within a clutter of words.

Conclusion

Delivering a rhetorical speech is the consummation of a long process that begins not with an "idea" but with a response to a situation. Rhetoric draws its energy from its surroundings and puts it into a form capable of mobilizing public audiences to act in such a way that corrects that situation, in either the long or the short term. By "form," then, we do not simply mean a pre-given shape, like a template or shell. Form means the ability to rouse the interests, energies, and appetites of an audience, to carry them through a logical and narrative structure from one place to another, and to bring together elements in such a way that satisfies these interests and leaves a lasting impression on the mind, imagination, and emotions. A good rhetorical speech therefore constructs a message that produces "form" in the psychology of the audience by giving form to a previously unformed situation, an act that produces both pleasure and learning.

Discussion Questions

1   Think of a speech introduction like a movie trailer. What recent trailers have you seen that "got attention and interest"? Do you think these are applicable to speeches?
2   What types of more traditional media, such as novels, poems, documentaries, movies, and the like, follow different patterns of arrangement?
3   What are some of the most memorable endings to stories you have read? Can you recall, from memory, famous "closing lines" of a movie or novel?
4   Think of speech parodies that appear in comedic political satire shows that intentionally are supposed to sound absurd. What rules of arrangement do they tend to violate?
5   Can you think of a "thesis," whether from history or from literature and film, that was phrased so eloquently that it became something of a maxim?
6   How might the subject "going out on a date" be organized differently using chronological, problem-solution, topical, logical, spatial, or pro-con arrangement?
7   How do people in ordinary social conversations get the attention and interest of their friends when they are about to tell a story. Can you think of any successful tactics?

Exercises

1   **Diverse arrangement**: As a class, come up with a specific purpose. After dividing the class into groups or individuals, assign a different strategy of introduction, organizing main points, and conclusion for everyone. Compose a brief speech according to their assigned arrangement. Compare and contrast the speeches and discuss how the different forms of arrangement influenced the type of speech that was given.
2   **Movie trailer**: Have everyone select one of their favorite movies. Now create your own rhetorical movie trailer that uses only words to get people to see the movie. Use the tactics of introduction and conclusion and select one form of arranging main points. As a trailer, the goal is not to summarize the whole movie. It is rather to bring out unique elements of the plot to make people interested.
3   **Storytelling**: The methods of arrangement can also be used simply to tell a good story. Take any experience from your own life and retell it by adapting it to fit the arrangement patterns. Retell the story using these methods but without calling attention to them. Afterwards, see if your audience can identify the method of arrangement being used.

6 Style

Style is the art of putting words together in such a way that it adds up to an attractive and meaningful unity. To appreciate the importance of style, one must overcome certain presumptions about style that tend to think of it in terms of "mere decoration," something that is insubstantial and simply added to the outside. However, if we look at our choices that we make in our everyday life, we realize that style matters a great deal. We invest considerable energy in how we choose to dress, eventually accumulating a wardrobe in which we will have a style for every occasion that matters to us. Our clothing style has a significant impact on the impression that we make to others and how this impression informs our subsequent relationship with them. We also know that our style impacts how we feel about ourselves. In other words, our style of dress changes the "substance" of our speech and behavior, and directly affects the way others respond to us.

The same is true with public speaking. When we attend to style, we often find that our choices of metaphors or speech patterns begin to have a direct impact on the very arguments we are making. Not only does attention to style make a speech more attractive to an audience, but it literally changes the content of the speech itself. In short, although style is often thought of simply as "ornamentation," the Latin term *ornare* is substantive and means "to equip, fit out, or supply." A soldier was thus "ornamented" with the weapons of war, meaning that a soldier without style was not, in fact, prepared to fight as a soldier. Similarly, rhetorical **style** is not the frivolous decoration of ideas; it is the filling out and forming of ideas in order to allow them to stand on their own and organize themselves as a coherent whole. With respect to the notion of form as the arousing and satisfying of the appetites of the audience, style represents the unique manner in which a speaker guides an audience through a speech and makes transitions between different items gathered through invention and then structured through arrangement. Style represents specific elements of the speech designed to capture the attention and seduce the ear of the audience, thereby making it engaged with what is being said and creating more of a feeling of continuity and unity. Style focuses on providing short, refined, effective parts of a speech that give clarity and power to specific ideas or images.

DOI: 10.4324/9781003316787-6

Style focuses on the uses of what are called **figures of speech**, which are words or phrases that are used in a way that create clarity, interest, or rhetorical effect. There are two types of figures of speech we will focus on in this chapter: schemes and tropes. A **scheme** is an artful deviation from the ordinary arrangement of words that emphasizes their sound and rhythm. For instance, the phrase "four score and seven years ago" in the Gettysburg Address is memorable because of the poetic patterns and the repetition of sounds. A **trope** is an artful deviation from the ordinary or principal signification of words that illuminates new forms of meanings and associations. When Abraham Lincoln says that "our fathers brought forth on this continent, a new nation, conceived in Liberty," he uses metaphors of conception and birth to discuss the origins of the nation in order to view the country as if it was a living organism.

Tropes highlight the fact that words do not simply have one precise meaning. Even a casual look at the dictionary shows a variety of different meanings any word can have depending on context. But the breadth of meaning goes even beyond multiple dictionary definitions. One can think of a word as having three potential meanings. First, the **denotative meaning** is analogous to the dictionary definition and represents the "thing" to which a word conventionally and objectively refers. For instance, the term "dog" used in a veterinary classroom denotes a canine. Second, the **connotative meaning** represents both the corresponding feelings and associated objects called forth by the word that often relate to a person's subjective life experience or cultural patterns. For instance, the phrase "doggie," even if it might denote a canine, has a positive connotative meaning associated with friendly, cute family pets. When searching for the connotative meaning, think about what people, objects, events, or actions are associated with a word without actually being the literal reference. Then consider the overall tone of this meaning and whether it has a positive or negative quality.

In order to help an audience to grasp precisely the intended denotative and connotative meanings in a vivid way, the first element of style on which to focus is the use of concrete words. A **concrete word** refers to tangible, qualities, characteristics, actions, or events that we can know through our senses and quickly visualize in our imagination. One should use clear and powerful words whenever possible, avoiding whenever possible not only empty pronouns like "it" or "this" or "they," but also vague adjectives like "good" or "bad" and inactive verbs like "is" or "was." That is to say, usually when people think of concrete words, they think of nouns. For instance, the noun *the red table* is preferable to the pronoun *it*, the word *Brazil* is preferable to *country*, or the word *fire ants* is more concrete than *insects*. However, it is important to point out that a concrete word does not refer only to nouns. One could start by saying, "The large Amazon rainforest is in Brazil." But the adjective "large" is very general, and "is" conveys no action. So you might try "The *sprawling* Amazon rainforest *covers* much of Brazil." Without concrete words, the denotative reference becomes too vague and the connotative meaning is diffuse or nonexistent. Consider the statement "It is big." The audience neither knows to what this refers nor particularly cares.

Lastly, the third type of meaning is presentational meaning. The **presentational meaning** of words relates purely to the impact of the sound or appearance of the words, like musical notes, quite apart from any meaningful reference. Presentational meaning has a strictly emotional reference, similar to how minor notes in a blues scale brings about different emotions than the clear progressions of a major scale. Simply by humming the words "Dog, doggie, dog" in sequential rhythm eventually strips the words of denotative and connotative meaning until they become simply a pattern of sounds. Or take the casual phrase, "He was a good old dog." It is hard not to say the words "good old dog" without a long stress on the word "old."

Just as concrete words help evoke denotative and connotative meanings, a focus on rhythm helps produce the musical aspect of presentational meaning. Rhythm in public speaking is how words "flow" through time. When we think of our natural environment, we might think of the rhythm of ripples on a lake or even the rhythm of a mountain range as one looks across the horizon. Replace ripples and mountain peaks with words and syllables and you understand how rhythm functions in public speaking. To use **rhythm** in rhetoric is to compose words that, when spoken and heard, follow musical pattern that is recognizable and predictable and helps an audience move along with the words. Lincoln, for instance, could have said "Eighty-seven years ago." But instead, he said "four score and seven years ago" because of the rhythmic pattern it produced. Rhythms act like threads that hold words together in a certain sequence which makes them easier to store in the filing cabinets of our memory. A speech with rhythm thus generally starts on a tension, rises to a climax, and comes to some resolution, carrying the audience along the whole time on a continuous flow.

Schemes

A scheme is an artful deviation from the normal structure and pattern of words. Schemes focus on rhythm and rhyme, repetitions of vowel and consonant sounds, and sequences of syllables. We interpret schemes more as sounds than as meanings, looking at sentences as bars in a musical score. Schemes set the tone for the occasion as well as placing the audience in a certain frame of mind to receive the message. It is a commonly known fact that messages tend to be recalled with greater clarity and emotional weight when they have a sense of rhythm and rhyme. The fact that complex song lyrics are easier to remember than clear but abstract definitions indicate the power of figures to leave a lasting impression. The same message conveyed without figures has a far greater chance of being forgotten than the one that was composed by a speaker who took the time to listen carefully to the sound of language with a musical ear. Although there are dozens of different schemes, the following are the most important schemes that appear in rhetoric.

Alliteration

If rhythm is a connecting thread, alliteration is like a hammered nail. **Alliteration** is the use of words that begin with the same consonant sound. Punctuating the same consonant sound "hammers" individual words into our memories. For example, the sentence "We delved into the dark dungeon of the deep" has a more memorable pattern than "We walked into the dark of the tunnel." However, alliteration is only effective when it is used with words that are worth remembering and emphasizing. The sentence "Tim's tie is too tight" has alliteration, but because the words are somewhat trivial, it sounds more comedic than profound. By contrast, a good speaker will alliterate words of importance that also fall on rhythmic "downbeats." For instance, "let us strive not for power but for peace and prosperity" emphasizes all of the key terms in the speech that are important and memorable. Keep in mind also that alliteration is more effective at the concluding and climactic parts of a speech that warrant emphasis. One should use alliteration during those parts of the speech that one wishes to truly emphasize one's point.

Repetition

There is a reason that advertising tends to say the same thing repeatedly—it trains the mind to associate certain meanings with certain objects, events, or people. As a figure, however, repetition is not simply repeating the same idea or claim; **repetition** is the repeated use of a key phrase to begin a series of sentences whose endings vary. For example, "We strive for independence. We strive for freedom. We strive for justice. And that is why we strive for nationhood." As with alliteration, effective use of repetition will emphasize key ideas and terms that also contain a certain rhythm. The phrase "We strive" not only establishes the character of the people as desiring something better, but it also fits into a sentence structure that has a rhythm that builds up to a conclusion. Like the climactic finale of a symphony, the phrases are structured so that *nationhood* is the final consummation of their struggles for independence, freedom, and justice. However, rhetorical use of repetition should only be used when the statement being repeated represents one of the key ideas of a speech. The repeated phrase should have a style and meaning itself that makes it worth remembering.

Parallelism

The figure of parallelism is more complicated than the earlier figures because it involves putting a longer string of words within a coherent structure that also conveys a balanced meaning. **Parallelism** is the repeated pairing of different, usually opposing, ideas in a rhythmic "couplet" within the same sentence. A rhythmic "couplet" is simply two ideas expressed in the same rhythm connected by an "and" or an "or." For example, "my blood or my tears" is a couplet, as is "the greatest of fears and the weakest of hopes" as is "the life of glory or the death of shame" as is "good and evil." Parallelism simply strings several of these couplets together in a single sentence. For example, "I see before us a choice between the hopes of millions and the fears of a few, the poverty of the many and the wealth of the one, and the progress of humanity and the debasement of mankind." By pairing opposite ideas or outcomes, it graphically presents the audience with a stark choice. However, it can equally be used to *bridge* opposites, as in the statement "Whether you were born within its borders or arrived on its shores, you are all Americans." In either case, parallelism operates most effectively when there are two distinct ideas or images which are being compared or contrasted.

Antithesis

An even more complex form of parallelism is antithesis. **Antithesis** is when two similarly phrased, but contradictory, ideas are consecutively expressed to favor one over the other. For example: "We live in a nation where laws are the rulers of men, not where men are the abusers of law." Antithesis is a form of parallelism in that it employs a rhythmic couplet, but it is more difficult to construct because the words must be carefully chosen so that they can be manipulated for the opposite effect. Putting together an antithesis is a lot like creating a puzzle, and its effectiveness is explained in the pleasure an audience gets from "solving" it. Ideas expressed in an antithesis should carry great weight, for otherwise an antithesis will sound more like a pun than a principle. To create an antithesis, simply take any phrase and try to find a similar wording that conveys the opposite idea or tendency that, when combined, creates a whole thought. The classic antithesis in presidential rhetoric is from John F. Kennedy, when he said "ask not what your country can do for you, but what you can do for your country." Keep in mind, too, that opposites need not be competitive. For instance, the golden rule is also an antithesis: "Do unto others as you would have them do unto you." In this case, the opposition is complementary, with each side supporting the other. The antithesis thus creates a sense of cooperation where before there were two forces going in different directions. Like other forms of style, antithesis often works best when "punctuating" a thought at the end of an argument.

Tropes

Tropes differ from figures in so far as they appeal more directly to the rational imagination than they do to the musical ear or rhythmic body. Tropes are useful because they encourage an audience to discern the meaning behind signs, thus generating a pleasure in participation very similar to the effects of a good puzzle or a riddle. For instance, the statement "the ocean's roar" is meaningful to us even though we know that the ocean cannot literally roar. The mind realizes that the two objects cannot be synonymous, so it starts sifting through other possible connotative meanings that might help us make sense of it. The harder and more difficult the trope, the harder the mind has to work to discern its meaning. This can increase the pleasure and level of participation in an audience when it reaches the correct level of difficulty, but beyond that it becomes too much labor and thereby acts as a repellent to the audience members, who will turn their attention to other things. Writing tropes that convey the correct meaning and challenge the audience at the ideal level is a most difficult art.[1] The rhetorical influence comes not from how it sounds or feels but how the words bring up ideas in the minds that are counterintuitive, surprising, distorted, exaggerated, amusing, or puzzling. The rest of the section will look at five of the more significant tropes, that of metaphor, simile, synecdoche, metonymy, and irony.

Hyperbole

One of the simplest tropes is that of **hyperbole**, which uses extreme exaggeration to highlight a specific quality or idea by making it seem larger than it actually is. An example of hyperbole might be, "When my father yelled at me, I could feel the whole house shake." Conversely, the trope of **litotes** uses understatement to make something seem smaller, as in the common phrase, "don't worry, it's just a scratch." However, because it tends to magnify something way out of proportion, hyperbole generally has a lot more persuasive power than litotes because we remember large things more than we do that which is small. To make use of hyperbole, you need simply take the quality you are most concerned with emphasizing in something, magnify it, find another thing in the world that is that size, and then use that as a comparison. For instance, stories about catching the Big Fish might use hyperbole, as in "that fish was as big as a whale" or that "it was so big it virtually sank the boat." Usually, hyperbole accompanies expansive hand gestures and an increase in volume and pitch.

Metaphor

To use metaphor is to give an audience a unique and creative perspective on some object, person, idea, or event in order to highlight specific qualities. A **metaphor** describes one thing by using language that is normally used to describe something seemingly unrelated to identify and communicate some shared quality. The simplest type of metaphor is a definition or comparison. Metaphors rely on comparing two terms with different denotative meanings, but which share similar connotative meanings. For example, to say "This meeting is a circus" is not to be taken literally. Rather, one abstracts a specific

1   See I. A. Richards, *The Philosophy of Rhetoric* (Oxford: Oxford University Press, 1936).

quality of a circus—its chaotic and unproductive character—and carries it over into the meeting.

But the best metaphors avoid the simple structure of "X is Y." Metaphor occurs any time we replace conventional description with words traditionally used for a different type of object. For instance, much of our metaphorical language comes from our creative use of verbs rather than any explicit comparison. If one wanted to describe a meeting as a circus, one might say "this clown is trying to juggle too many balls." There is no explicit comparison here. Instead, the subject is assumed and then the description simply treats the subject "as if" it was a clown. Metaphors are often more effective in this way because they are less explicit and appeal more subtly to the imagination. In addition, to use Aristotelian terms, they put the image "before the eyes" and make them "move" or "come alive." It is more visual to imagine the chairperson of the board as a juggling clown than the more general comparison of a circus. When we use metaphors, it is better to make these images come alive by using active verbs and adjectives rather than simply comparing two objects using the verb "to be."

One form of metaphor that is particularly useful is **personification**, which describes abstract or nonhuman objects as if they possessed human qualities. In the previous examples, we saw a comparison of an object with an object (a meeting and a circus) and a person with a person (a chairperson and a clown). Personification simply describes the character of a nonhuman object as if it had human or animate qualities. For instance, "this meeting crawled on and on" describes the meeting as if it were a creature. Personification can be very effectively paired with concrete words as well. Specifying which aspect of a thing one is talking about, and then animating that part using personification, can very effectively bring the image of that thing to mind, much as cartoons give personalities to inanimate objects in a way that make them memorable.

Simile

Similes are similar to metaphors, but they are more explicit in their comparison and often explain the reason why this comparison is being made. We often think of the defining quality of a simile as a comparison that uses the words "like" or "as." For instance, "terrorism is a cancer" is considered a metaphor while "terrorism *spreads like* a cancer" is considered a simile. This is generally true, but focusing exclusively on these minor grammatical differences misses the more important difference. Unlike metaphors, **similes** highlight a specific quality of a thing by *explicitly* comparing it to a similar and defined quality in something unrelated. For example, the second example specifically indicates that terrorism is a cancer because it possesses the same quality of "spreading." It does not leave it simply up to the imagination but indicates why, explicitly, the comparison is being made. By contrast, metaphors often leave it up to the audience to make the connection between the two things being compared. Similes do the job for it.

Similes limit the range of possible interpretations in order to reduce miscommunication. They are therefore helpful in settings of instruction, particularly technical or scientific instruction concerning complicated relationships where a clear message needs to be conveyed by using simple examples. Parents thus often employ similes with children ("The moon shines because it reflects like a mirror"), whereas they employ metaphors with their adult friends in casual conversation ("My old car was a lemon."). The drawback is that they also tend to have less impact because the audience isn't as involved in the creative process. A good metaphor is like a good joke—the audience should be able to "get it" without too much explanation. Similes are like offering explanations to your jokes so that people understand them. When looking to make a dramatic impact with unexpected imagery, use metaphors. But when you want to expound on a particular comparison to make your message clear, a simile can be very effective.

Synecdoche

Whereas a metaphor is a way of gaining perspective on something by looking at it in a unique and different way, a **synecdoche** is a way of representing a larger complete whole by describing it only in terms of a smaller part that stands in for it. In its most traditional form, a synecdoche simply describes an object by using a term for its most recognizable "part." For instance, before the invention of the steamship, people would use the term "sail" to stand for ships, as in "the merchant possesses 30 sail." Today, phrases like "we need more *boots* on the ground" (the boot being just a part of a soldier) or "I would like another pair of *hands* over here" (meaning a person who can help do something physically with their hands) or "that's a nice set of *wheels*!" (to indicate a car or motorcycle) are all common uses of synecdoche. In the traditional sense, the important part of synecdoche is finding the *essential* and most *representative* part of the object being described in order to best convey what is significant about it.

However, a synecdoche also refers to anything which "stands in" for a whole as a literal representative. In other words, sometimes the "part" can be an individual amidst a group, as for instance a congressional representative is a synecdoche for his or her district or the testimony of a Holocaust survivor represents in general form the experiences of all Holocaust survivors. Similarly, any graphic representation of a complex environment that simplifies it using a "microcosm" is also a synecdoche. Think, for instance, of stereotypic typical treasure maps in which only specific key features of an environment are highlighted in order to guide someone to a buried chest. All these aspects are simplified representations, or parts, of the whole. In these cases, one must choose the essential features of an object that genuinely capture its essential and most prominent qualities. In this way synecdoche is related to the argument by example, when a single story, individual, or event is representative of a larger narrative, community, or history.

Metonymy

Conventionally understood, a metonymy is when something is not called by its own name, but with some object associated with it. For instance, a traditional example of a metonymy might be a "badge" to stand in for a police officer, or a "tiara" to stand in for a princess. However, this way of interpreting metonymy overlaps too much with synecdoche insofar as a badge can also be considered a "part" of an officer's uniform or a tiara a "part" of a princess. The difference is subtle but important. Strictly speaking, a metonymy using a badge or a tiara would actually be standing in for the *idea* of "law and order" or of "monarchy," not a specific person. To understand this difference, let us turn to the definition of metonymy. If a metaphor is a *perspective* on something by using language usually reserved for something else, and a synecdoche is a *representation* of a whole of something through a part of it, then a metonymy is the *reduction* of an idea by naming it as if it were an object.

Specifically, **metonymy** is a way we represent a purely abstract idea, a motion, or concept by treating it as if it was a purely physical existence. The function of metonymy, therefore, is to help us tangibly grasp and visually represent something which would otherwise be very difficult to communicate. For instance, one of the most frequent expressions of metonymy is the picture of a red heart to symbolize "love." To return to the example of the badge, therefore, it is a synecdoche if the badge is being used to stand in for the physical person to whom it belongs—as one might see a badge on the ground as evidence that a police officer had been there. The key difference with metonymy is that the badge is not being used to represent a specific individual or even a group of police officers, but the *abstract idea of law and order in general*, as in the television show *The Badge*. For instance, a more explicit and common use of metonymy is the notion of balanced scales to represent "justice." The essential quality of metonymy, therefore, is that the object being represented has no other physical existence beyond its representation. It exists only as an "idea" or "abstraction." Many of our most powerful symbols are those that represent the abstract ideals of the nation (such as a flag) or the virtues of a religion (such as the cross, star, or crescent) and so therefore must be treated with particular care. But metonymy can be very effective in bringing together a community.

Irony

The last and perhaps most complex of the major tropes is irony. **Irony** highlights the contradiction between expectation and reality, or between what is literally expressed and what is intended. Sarcasm, for instance, is a basic form of irony. If someone trips and falls, and another person says "well that was graceful!" the apparent (or literal) meaning of the words is clearly the opposite of its actual meaning. Irony thus has a "dialectical" character, meaning that it always contains two opposing ideas. In the case of this example of sarcasm, the literal idea might be "you did something very graceful." But with sarcasm, the literal meaning is inverted, so that one also hears the phrase "you did something very clumsy." The resulting meaning is the interaction between these two competing statements. One of the reasons that it is difficult to convey sarcasm in writing, for instance, is that writing lacks the nonverbal cues that tells us to invert the meaning. What might be intended as a joke on a text message is then interpreted literally by the receiver and misunderstanding results.

But there is far more to irony than just sarcasm, which generally one should avoid in a public speech. Irony is more persuasive when one reveals an unexpected meaning, contradiction, or outcome. There are two types of irony one can employ in public speaking. The most common type is **verbal irony**, in which case one says the opposite of what one actually means. More often than not, this is most effective when used to produce laughter by indirectly referencing a fact which is common knowledge to a friendly audience. Verbal irony in front of a hostile audience almost always fails. A more complex type of irony to use is **situation irony**, in which someone's actions produced the very opposite effect than what they had intended. In this case, the speaker has to narrate a particular situation and show how certain choices that had been made to bring about a certain goal had in fact made the opposite thing occur. Sometimes this is used for comic effect, as when the best laid plans go askew. Other times it is used to criticize one's opponents, showing how their poor judgment produced the opposite outcomes.

Conclusion

Style is what gives a speech its character, spirit, and life. Speeches are memorable because they have style. Often, even the most well-argued points are difficult to recall after time has passed. But when the vivid imagery of a trope is combined with the rhythmic patterns of a scheme, it can leave an impact on the mind that creates a memory capable of vivid recall. Ralph Waldo Emerson highlights this particular quality of style to condense the meaning and power of a speech into a few phrases:

> The orator must be, to a certain extent, a poet. We are such imaginative creatures that nothing so works on the human mind, barbarous or civil, as a trope. Condense some daily experience into a glowing symbol, and an audience is electrified. They feel as if they already possessed some new right and power over a fact which they can detach, and so completely master in thought. It is a wonderful aid to the memory, which carries away the image and never loses it … Put the argument into a concrete shape, into an image—some hard phrase, round and solid as a ball, which they can see and handle and carry home with them—and the cause is half-won.[2]

2 Ralph Waldo Emerson, "Eloquence," https://emersoncentral.com/essays/eloquence (accessed March 24, 2022).

Emerson here perfectly captures the purpose of style: to put an argument into a hard phrase, round and solid as a ball that the audience can carry home with them. Of course, this action also requires leaving out many details and accepting that an audience cannot carry everything home. Style focuses on those key elements in the speech that you want to make memorable. The hope is that they can use these few parts of the speech as reminders of the larger whole, encouraging them to return to the fuller speech to seek out the more carefully reasoned sections when the situation demands. Style is thus the gateway to logic, smoothing the way to persuasion.

Discussion Questions

1   The appeal of schemes seems rooted in our sensory apparatus. Where can you see parallels to schemes with how birds and animals communicate with one another?
2   One can also think of schemes in terms of how we communicate with babies. How do the sounds we make to babies reflect certain aspects of schemes?
3   What famous nursery rhymes or popular poems, like limericks, make use of schemes to make them easy to remember and attractive to the ear?
4   What advertising slogans or "jingles" can you think of that use schemes to great effect?
5   What are some common metonymies that we see every day that use specific objects to stand in either for abstract ideas and emotions or general groups and organizations?
6   How does a map, a congressional representative, a piece of clothing, or a tourist trip all function as a synecdoche in different ways?
7   Metaphors are often borrowed from new technology to describe human relationships. What metaphors do we use today that reflect our obsession with digital technology?
8   Why is irony so difficult to communicate on text messaging compared with face-to-face conversation? What ways do we use to communicate irony through text, and how do these actions illuminate the nature of irony?

Exercises

1   **Haiku**: Compose a short haiku poem about something you experienced in the past day. A conventional haiku is structured by three lines that have a syllable structure of 5-7-5. The first two lines should concentrate on a graphic description of something simple, usually a phenomenon in nature, while the last line should comment more broadly on the meaning or emotional significance of this experience. Focus on the use of concrete words, rhythm, alliteration, and metaphor, and do not use any pronouns or the words "is" or "was."

2 **Sentence revision**: Begin with the sentence: "Now is the time to put a stop to that." Write it on the board. First, step by step, replace each word or phrase with a more concrete word or phrase. Second, intentionally add schemes to improve rhythm and rhyme. Third, use a trope to give it a deeper meaning. Now practice different ways of delivering this sentence.

3 **Encomium of the ordinary**: Identify an ordinary object that you have in your possession. Write a 5-sentence oration praising this object using schemes and tropes. Make sure to exaggerate its importance. Try to push language to its limit in order to make this object seem like a rare and special item that enriches your life.

References

Emerson, Ralph Waldo. "Eloquence," https://emersoncentral.com/essays/eloquence/ (accessed March 24, 2022).

Richards, I. A. *The Philosophy of Rhetoric* (Oxford: Oxford University Press, 1936).

7   Ethos

Perhaps what most distinguishes public speaking from any other form of persuasion is the fact that its effectiveness relies so heavily on the character of the speaker. A public speaker steps before the members of an audience and effectively asks them a favor, to listen attentively as the speaker rewards their time and energy with a speech that is tailored specifically to their interests. Even in digital social influencing, a speaker must engage an audience immediately and demonstrate that most treasured commodity—that of authenticity—to keep them from moving on to more interesting material. When we decide to be a member of an audience, whether virtually or in person, we do so because we want to listen to the *speaker*, and we have done so because we have put trust in that speaker to reward our time commitment. Any successful public speech must therefore begin with the existence of mutual trust that forms a temporary relationship between speaker and audience. Without a sense of this "bond," a speaker's words are just more data.

For the purposes of rhetorical public speech, **ethos** represents this sense of public character that is recognized by an audience and influences their reception of the speaker's arguments. Ethos is the capacity to influence an audience based on the audience's perceptions of the credibility and character of the speaker in relationship to the audience's own interests and values. Ethos in the rhetorical sense is therefore not something absolute, stable, and private that one carries around wherever one goes; it is determined by the relationship one has with an audience through action and performance. To understand the possible effects of one's rhetoric, then, a person must understand how an audience perceives his or her character. For the Greeks, people with ethos were those people who earned respect, admiration, and allegiance through both word and deed. The concept of ethos has distinctly rhetorical implications because it deals with aspects of credibility and authority that influence our choice of whom to trust when faced with important decisions. Because we often do not have the time or resources to be able to make crucial judgments on our own, we look to those who possess strength of character, or ethos, to help guide our actions. For this reason, Aristotle believed that among the three forms of rhetorical proof (ethos, pathos, and logos), ethos was often the most powerful. He writes:

DOI: 10.4324/9781003316787-7

There is persuasion through character whenever the speech is spoken in such a way as to make the speaker worthy of credence; for we believe fair-minded people to a greater extent and more quickly than we do others, on all subjects in general and completely so in cases where there is not exact knowledge but room for doubt. And this should result from the speech, not from a previous opinion that the speaker is a certain kind of person; for it is not the case as some of the handbook writers propose in their treatment of the art at fair-mindedness on the part of the speaker makes no contribution to persuasive this; rather, character is almost, so to speak, the most authoritative form of persuasion.[1]

The reason that ethos is the most authoritative form of persuasion is simply because we tend to accept the opinions of those people who we feel are more like us and who have our best interests at heart. Particularly when hundreds of different messages surround us every day, demanding our attention for this thing or that, ethos provides us an efficient and often (if not always) reliable way of selecting those few that we think are tailored specifically to our lives and our concerns. Ethos establishes a meaningful bond between speaker and audience and distills from the cacophony of popular and political culture a single message that creates a sense of shared experience between both speaker and audience and between audience members themselves.

Because it is so central to the act of public speaking, establishing ethos is a complex process that involves more than simply offering an audience a list of accomplishments and admirable characteristics. Developing ethos in a public speech is not the same as presenting a written resume for a job application. The goal of developing ethos is to establish a relationship, not to document facts. Aristotle explains the difficulty of establishing ethos and its three components:

> There are three reasons why speakers themselves are persuasive; for there are three things we trust other than logical demonstration. These are practical wisdom (*phronesis*), and virtue (*arête*), and goodwill (*eunoia*): for speakers make mistakes in what they say through failure to exhibit either, all, or one of these; for either through lack of practical sense they do not form opinions rightly; or through forming opinions they do not say what they think because of the bad character; or they are prudent and fair-minded but let goodwill, so that it is possible for people not to give the best advice although they know what it is. These are the only possibilities.[2]

1   Aristotle, *Rhetoric*, available at http://classics.mit.edu/Aristotle/rhetoric.1.i.html (accessed March 24, 2022), 1356a.
2   Aristotle, *Rhetoric*, 1358a.

Understanding the subtleties of Aristotle's argument requires a clear distinction between these three components of ethos.

1   **Practical wisdom** is the proven ability to size up problematic situations and make judgments that show prudence and forethought. It is a capacity to make the right decisions given many alternatives. For instance, at a job interview you might prove practical wisdom by talking about the many "tough choices" you had to make in times of high stress that proved to be the right move.

2   **Virtue** is an established habit of going good, of performing particular activities that are held in high regard and embody the best cultural values. Virtue in the Greek did not refer to some inner goodness; it meant "excellence," like we would refer to the virtues of an athlete, a musician, a parent, a leader, or a soldier. Thus, in an interview, one might refer to one's habits of performance, the fact that one works hard, shows up on time, and tells the truth.

3   **Goodwill** means the presence of conscious and thoughtful consideration of the audience's well-being, as we would expect from a good friend. Goodwill does not guarantee good advice or even good judgment. But it does ensure that a person has our best interests at heart. We might prove goodwill in an interview by how much volunteer work we do, our loyalty to our former employers, or our love of our profession.

In summary, we prove practical wisdom by boasting of our track record of past decisions, we prove virtue by showing how we have committed ourselves to certain noble habits of action, and we prove goodwill by addressing the concerns and interests of our audience and by revealing our willingness to sacrifice our own self-interest in service of their prosperity. The ideal is to demonstrate all three, but sometimes that may be difficult. For instance, a criminal may have demonstrated practical wisdom in his ability to rob banks, but lack virtue and goodwill. A reclusive monk might be well esteemed in virtue, but have little practical wisdom for everyday situations and perhaps might not care. And an old high school friend might have all the goodwill in the world toward you, but lack good sense and most components of virtue. In each case, we might have interesting conversations with each of these individuals, but rhetorically we would not necessarily look to them for counsel in times of crisis or uncertainty. It is during these times that ethos becomes a powerful persuasive tool because it focuses an audience's attention on the message that comes from one respected individual. Developing this rhetorical ethos will be the subject of the rest of this chapter.

Persona

Most people step into any familiar social situation with an **inherited ethos**, which is the actual reputation that rhetors "carry with them" because of an audience's acquaintance with past behavior. When an inherited ethos is well-established, such as the ethos of a mother for her child or that which close friends have with each other, a speaker rarely has to spend any time establishing his or her reputation or credibility. It certainly would be strange for a mother to say to her child, "Because I have worked hard these many years learning how to cook healthy meals (practical wisdom), because I care deeply for your future (goodwill), and because I am a just and honorable soul (virtue), please listen to my recommendation to eat your spinach." Having already established her ethos, she simply says "Eat your spinach." Inherited ethos is this kind of unspoken credibility that needs no mention to function. In Aristotle's language, it is **inartistic**, meaning something that one can just "point to" rather than craft through language, as in **artistic** proofs that require careful craft in a speech.

Ethos becomes a uniquely rhetorical concern of *art* only when rhetors, in some form, create or modify the perception of an audience about them. **Persona** is this rhetorical creation; it represents the constructed ethos that a rhetor creates within the confines of a particular rhetorical text. Persona, in other words, is more a creation of language rather than an inheritance of history. Like the costume that transforms an actor into a new personality on stage, rhetoric can create a "public face" that best suits the immediate needs of a rhetor. Unlike inherited ethos, which is the product of cumulative interactions or exposure over time with an audience, one's persona is always tied to a specific discourse and is completely contained within that discourse. For example, a convict before a parole board enters the hearing with an inherited ethos as a liar and a thief, and he attempts to counter that reputation by describing himself as a "changed man" who has seen the error of his ways. The decision of the board rests on whether the convict's persona of a "changed man" is more convincing than the inherited ethos of a liar and a thief.

Deciding when to construct a persona and when to rely on the strength of one's inherited ethos depends upon the presence and quality of one's reputation within an audience. On the one hand, when a speaker is unknown to an audience, creating a persona is necessary in order to present a favorable "first impression."[3] We are all familiar with our first job interviews when we had to define ourselves as an ideal employee. On the other hand, when a speaker enters a situation as a respected leader, there is no need for such self-promotion; indeed, it would be seen as being in bad taste. Rarely do we enjoy listening to famous and powerful people talking about their fame and power. But most speaking situations usually fall somewhere in between these two extremes. In these cases, one must construct a persona that somehow addresses, modifies, and transcends the limits of one's inherited ethos.

---

3   An interesting account of an actual scholarly persona is found in James Darsey, "Edwin Black and the First Persona," *Rhetoric & Public Affairs* 10, no. 3 (2007), 501–507.

Because the construction of personae deals not just with possession of knowledge or skills, but with notions of character, it relies heavily on personal stories and the form of delivery. **Personal stories** are narrations of one's life experience that provide insight into the speaker's practical wisdom, virtue, or goodwill. Phrases like "The time I was behind enemy lines ..." or "When I saved my sister's life ..." or "Growing up in a tough neighborhood ..." signify to an audience that a person is relating a story that offers a window into his or her deeper self. The **form of delivery** reveals character by using phrases, words, accents, or gestures commonly associated with certain character types. Hence, a president often vacillates between acting "presidential" by speaking in firm, calm, and authoritative terms in formal settings and behaving as an "ordinary American" by doing volunteer work with rolled-up sleeves and telling jokes around a barbeque. Form of delivery is important because we trust those who speak like us, not just because it is familiar, but because it shows a mastery of the type of language that can only be acquired through life experience. It is thus an expression of goodwill.

Although, strictly speaking, the personae available for a rhetor are infinite, there are nonetheless general types of personae that are always familiar and that conform to our social conventions. Take, for instance, just a few popular personae: the country lawyer, the wise sage, the teenage rebel, the religious prophet, the CEO, the father/mother figure, the loyal friend, the iconoclast, the president, the confidant, the drill sergeant, or the door-to-door salesperson. Any person attempting to create his or her own persona, of course, will always individualize his or her character such that no two personae will ever be alike. But in their review of the research on the roles typically played by rhetors in rhetorical situations, Roderick Hart and Susanne Daughton have identified four recurring personae that reoccur though speeches in different forms: the apologist, the agent, the partisan, and the hero.[4] These roles are not mutually exclusive. A speaker might combine different characteristics within a single speech. However, they are each helpful to isolate a particular attitude that you might adopt when making a suitable point.

1   You might adopt the role of **apologist** when you wish to rebuff an attack either on yourself or a group or institution to which you belong. The essential characteristic of the apologist is *righteous indignation*. The apologist does not actually "apologize." Like Socrates in front of the jury, the apologist instead corrects the mistaken impression of the audience and seeks to clarify the essential rightness of his or her position.

2   The **agent** speaks on behalf of some institution as a spokesperson of legitimate authority, thereby standing as a "representative" of a recognized institution or social group. The essential characteristic of the agent is *enthusiastic loyalty* typical of politicians, priests, presidents,

4   Roderick Hart and Susanne Daughton, *Modern Rhetorical Criticism*, 3rd ed. (Boston, MA: Pearson, 2005), 220–221.

chancellors, community leaders, social movement activists, and ambassadors of all kinds. You would adopt a persona of agent when all of your arguments point back to the group to which you belong, rather than taking credit for things yourself.

3   The **partisan** is one who represents not a group or institution but an idea or ideal. The essential characteristic of the partisan is *critical idealism*. Partisan are idealists because they are advocating a vision of society or politics or religion that is not yet real but that might be possible with faith and effort; and they are critical because in order to make this possibility a reality, they must remove many obstacles in the path, obstacles that are usually tied to tradition, law, or institutional inertia. Whereas agents take pride in the group to which they long, partisans point upward to the ideas that inspire them.

4   Finally, the **hero** is defined as an individual who is willing to actively confront power in the name of helping others even if it means that great suffering might come upon him or her. The essential characteristic of the hero is therefore *romantic courage*. Heroes are "romantic" because, unlike the partisan, they do not have a coherent political vision they are promoting, but instead boldly stride into the unknown against all obstacles with the optimistic faith that things will work out for them in the end. And unlike agents, they do not have to speak "on behalf" of the group they defend. They act only on their own impulses, but they do so in defense of the vulnerable.

Some of the greatest orations combined many or even all of these roles, with the speaker taking on new personae during different phases of the speech. For instance, an American president might assume the role of the *apologist* in defense of the wisdom of some military policy ("Those who question the wisdom of toppling this dictator do not properly understand the nature of evil"), then might take on the role of *agent* ("As the commander-in-chief of this nation, I will not allow its foreign policy to be determined by petty tyrants"), only to then transition to being a *partisan* ("Furthermore, this campaign is not simply about our national self-interest; I advocate this policy not simply because I am president, but because I believe that the true task of humanity is to spread freedom and democracy around the globe") and then end on a *heroic* note ("Finally, I can no longer stand to see children suffer and mothers weep; when evil shows its face it must be confronted at all costs if we are to live with ourselves"). A role is not something that locks us permanently into any type of performance; it is a type of script we perform to accomplish a specific rhetorical task.

Evoked Audience

If the persona is the image that the rhetor constructs of him- or herself as a speaker, the **evoked audience** is the attractive image that the rhetor constructs of and for the audience. If the speaker's constructed self-image can be considered as the "first" persona (in which the speaker tells the audience who "I" am), then the evoked audience can be considered as the "second" persona (in which the speaker tells the audience who "they" are). The concept of the second persona was advanced by Edwin Black. For him, an astute rhetorical critic can thus see "in the auditor implied by a discourse a model of what the rhetor would have his real auditor become."[5] The function of the evoked audience, or this "second persona," is to create an attractive image of unity that makes members of an audience desire to be a part of a common group rather than an aggregate of separate individuals.

In its most general form, we find politicians using evoked audiences whenever they speak of the *American people* as a collective body of people who love liberty, freedom, and democracy. By creating a category of identity that can unify a group of separate individuals, an evoked audience creates the possibility of cooperative action because it contributes to the creation of a sense of unity that may not have existed before the speech. For example, we often take for granted that everyone who is born within the geographic boundaries of the United States is an "American," but prior to the revolution, people identified themselves more with their local city or region. For revolutionaries to start using the term *American* thus helped make possible a national identity that stood apart from the British Empire.[6] So a revolutionary speaker trying to "evoke" an audience at this time might use an argument like "You lovers of liberty! You fighters for Freedom! You are not members of states and cities. You are Americans!" This would invite the audience to embrace a common identity they did not previously accept.

Like the concept of persona, the evoked audience is a partly fictional identity that usually overstates the unified character of the people listening to a speech (who in reality are far more diverse). Like persona, the evoked audience often is what a rhetor *wants* an audience to be rather than what it literally *is*. Yet this ideal often brings a new reality into existence. For instance, a collection of teenagers may all be talented at a certain sport, but they do not think of themselves as a "team" until the coach starts telling them to act like one ("Go Tigers!"). The coach's rhetoric creates a sense of commonality by evoking the team spirit within the individual players that may not have been fully present before. The most typical sign that such a team spirit is being attempted by a speaker is the repetitive use of "we" or "you," such that an audience feels it is being grouped together under a single category. One can imagine a parent telling his or her children, "If we are a family, then we will eat together at the dinner table." The implicit choice now placed upon the audience is whether or not to accept that group membership.

5   Edwin Black, "The Second Persona," in *Readings in Rhetorical Criticism*, ed. Carl R. Burghardt (State College, PA: Strata Publishing Co., 1995), 90.
6   For more on the "public" as an evoked audience, see Michael McGee, "In Search of the People," *Quarterly Journal of Speech* 71 (1975), 235–249.

Therefore, although there is a fictional quality about an evoked audience, this does not mean that it is an illusion. Clearly, a speaker who speaks to an audience of school children as if they were all members of Congress is not literally accurate. However, motivational teachers *can* speak to them as "future leaders of America" and anticipate an energetic response. In other words, the evoked audience should always select and amplify shared qualities that are already present (or at least potentially present) within an audience. The average audience of college students, for instance, can be referred to as "university students," or "citizens," or "eager young people," or "future leaders," or "party-goers." Each of these designations may be partly true, but each of them only speaks to one portion of that group's identity. But for the time they are listening to the speech, the evoked audience allows them to participate in a feeling of common identity.

Identification

When we "identify" with someone, we see ourselves as sharing some quality or experience with another person or group. Usually, this feeling comes after the revelation of a life experience that we see as similar to our own. The process of making friends with people often begins with this step of identification in which two strangers find themselves sharing in some common interest, habit, belief, or feeling. In this sense, the process of identification is how two or more people come to form a bond that generates commonality out of what might seem, at first, to be different perspectives. What we "identify," then, is some quality in another person that he or she shares with us. Identification is not merely labeling something; it is identifying the qualities in others that we find in ourselves as well.

In rhetoric, **identification** is the strategy of creating a common bond between speaker and audience by pointing out and narrating the qualities, background, interests, and character that they share. For Kenneth Burke, *identification* is a broad term that ranges from the simple schoolyard attempt to make friends by asserting a common quality or interest (e.g., "we are all baseball lovers") to religious or nationalistic attempts to create a unified group with common goals and characteristics.[7] What each of these examples has in common is a sense that two or more distinct and unique individuals share in some "essence" or "quality" that transcends their individuality (love of farming, class identity, and divine origin, respectively). This sense of commonality thus leads to people uniting in a common purpose. Unlike the evoked audience, which concerns only the common qualities of the "you," identification represents the persuasive attempt on the part of the rhetorical agent to say "I am one of you" in order to create a sense of "we." The justification for such a strategy is that we tend to prefer listening to people

7   For more on identification, see Kenneth Burke, *A Rhetoric of Motives* (Berkeley, CA: University of California Press, 1969), xiv.

who feel and think like we do—particularly as it relates to how we think and feel about the subject matter we are talking about.[8]

Identification is perhaps the most important tool in building ethos in a speech. It is through methods of identification that the speaker and audience feel connected. This strategy is not simply something to use in the introduction, in which we might formally introduce ourselves to an audience. For instance, "It is good to be here talking with you young voters. I remember when I was in high school before I ran for Congress," and so on. Identification is more powerful when it is more subtly sprinkled throughout the speech anytime there is an opportunity to indicate a commonality not only between *speaker* and audience but also between *subject* and audience. For instance, if you are making a speech criticizing the horrible conditions of sweatshop labor to an audience that has never experienced any such condition and has no familiarity with the countries in which such labor occurs, you have to find a way to make them care about the subject and feel some sort of common interest in preventing exploitation. To do so, one can point to the clothes that people are wearing that might have come from such factories; one can portray the workers as if they are not strangers but individuals very much like people brothers or sisters; one can draw from more familiar experiences the audience have with labor to try to make them feel what it is like to work in one of these factories. By doing so, this creates a margin of overlap between subject and audience, which in turn creates a sense of identification with you, the speaker, insofar as all of you now share a common interest in regulating sweatshop labor. In other words, you create identification not simply by saying "you and I are alike" but rather by saying "you and I care about the same subject because it all touches us in some way." This is a far more subtle but lasting strategy to create identification.

Distinction

Identification is a mainstay of rhetorical persuasion, but it is not always sufficient. Especially in times of uncertainty, when we seek good advice rather than loyal friendship, we often look to those people who are very *unlike* us because they possess uncharacteristic excellence in character or special expertise in a very specific subject. In other words, we often want speakers not to "fit in" but to "stand out." In other words, in cases of *distinction*, the persona of the rhetor stands apart from the evoked audience; in cases of *identification*, it is aligned with it. Both represent forms of credibility, but distinction is credibility from *difference* (even if it is just difference in degree), whereas identification is credibility from *likeness*. Frequently, some combination of the two is most useful.[9]

8   For more on identification, see Gary C. Woodward, *The Idea of Identification* (Albany, NY: State University of New York Press, 2003).
9   The desirability of a mixture of both qualities is exemplified by the notion of "source credibility" as explained by Jack Whitehead in "Factors of Source Credibility," *Quarterly Journal of Speech* 54 (1968), 59–63.

A four-star general cites the possession of superior knowledge and broader experience in order to justify leading a campaign, but he or she usually makes an effort to also establish how he or she is still a common soldier "at heart" in order to command loyalty. Presidential candidates, too, often spend a great deal of time touting their expertise while simultaneously spending most of their days eating hot dogs, going bowling, or kissing babies. They want to appear as ordinary citizens and extraordinary leaders simultaneously.

In summary, **distinction** is the attempt to establish credibility by the possession of special knowledge and/or unique experience that are superior to those of the audience. **Special knowledge** refers to the kind of knowledge one receives by learning technical discourses and procedures, such as the knowledge one receives from attending a university. Whether experts are scientists, theologians, ethicists, economists, or movie critics, they all base their arguments on knowledge not accessible to the general public. **Unique experience** refers to the kind of expertise one acquires by having "been there" or "gone through that." For example, it is a common dramatic technique used in all war movies that the highly educated new officer always defers to the practical experience of the veteran soldier once combat begins. The officer might be more capable to discuss broader military strategy (thus having special knowledge), but the enlisted soldier usually knows better what to do in the heat of battle (thus possessing unique experience). The ideal, of course, is a fusion of both qualities within a single person.

Polarization

Understanding of the complex ethics behind strategies of ethos would not be complete without a consideration of polarization (or "division"). Just as any action has a reaction, any attempt to establish unity inevitably also creates a division between "in" groups and "out" groups that results in inevitable polarization. For something to be "polarized" is to have two objects that repel each other from a distance. For instance, the North Pole and the South Pole represent two sides of the earth, but they are not antagonistic toward one another. They are simply far apart. Two magnets of the same polarity, however, will literally repulse each other when brought together. Similarly, two friends separated by thousands of miles are not polarized, but simply distant; two enemies in the same room, however, will create a palpable tension. Polarization thus represents a division based on antagonism. For example, we are often forced to choose between aligning ourselves with one group or another with little room for compromise. Either we are "with them or against them." And those who seek compromise in this situation are thus usually attacked from both sides for being wishy-washy. In a polarized environment, the decision not to choose is also a choice that puts us at risk of being abandoned, rejected, or ignored.

By its nature as an art that thrives in conflict and uncertainty, rhetorical discourse often magnifies these choices and uses the contrast to force a decision. In rhetoric, **polarization** is the strategy of dividing an audience into a positive "us" and a negative "them" to create unity through difference. The "them" in this case is usually a **criticized audience** that represents a group antagonistic to the rhetor's interests, such as another political party, or simply a demonized audience that is used as a convenient foil, such as a group of "traitors" or "evil-doers." The strategy is then to argue that if one does not follow the path preferred by the rhetor (a path that ends in belonging to an evoked audience), then this person will align him- or herself with a group of people who lack ethical or practical judgment. This model can be applied effectively in the analysis of contemporary partisan politics.[10] In summary, if the first persona presents the "I" who is speaking and the second persona defines the "you" who is being spoken to, polarization defines a "third" persona representing the undesirable "they" who are not present but who are used to define who the "I" and "you" are not.[11]

Including "polarization" within a public speaking textbook may appear to border on the unethical. After all, are we not usually advised to invite as many people as possible to hear our speech? Is it not completely inappropriate in a tolerant age to pick out a group of people (or a type of person) to criticize or condemn? The work of Kenneth Burke is instructive here. Throughout his writings, Burke lamented the tendency for **scapegoating** in public rhetoric, in which all a public's "sins" are placed upon a largely defenseless group that is then run out of town. At the same time, however, Burke also recognized that division is a natural state of human nature, and that rhetoric arises whenever individuals and groups are in conflict with one another. Moreover, rhetorical action cannot avoid the effects of polarization. For instance, even the statement "we should all love one another" can be used to divide those who love from those who hate. Burke's point is that we must be aware of the implicit acts of polarization that occur in all our identifications, make them explicit, and do our best to make our criticisms of others intelligent, precise, just, and sympathetic.

One common strategy to make polarization less ethically problematic is to base it more on hypothetical values or attitudes than on actual characteristics of specific social groups. Certainly, parents who ask their children whether they want to be a "doctor" or a "couch potato" are using polarization primarily to inspire them to do their best. In this case, the negative audience

---

10 Some examples discussing the rhetoric of polarization include Andrew King and Floyd Douglas Anderson, "Nixon, Agnew, and the 'Silent Majority': A Case Study in the Rhetoric of Polarization," *Western Speech* 35, no. 4 (1971), 243–255; William D. Harpine, "Bryan's 'A Cross of Gold': The Rhetoric of Polarization at the 1896 Democratic Convention," *Quarterly Journal of Speech* 87, no. 3 (2001), 291–304; and David E. Foster, "Bush's Use of the Terrorism and 'Moral Values' Issues in His 2004 Presidential Campaign Rhetoric: An Instance of the Rhetorical Strategy of Polarization," *Ohio Communication Journal* 44 (2006), 33–60.

11 See Philip Wander, "The Third Persona: An Ideological Turn in Rhetorical Theory," *Central States Speech Journal* 35 (1984), 197–216.

is not real but hypothetical—it represents a "type" of behavior we find distasteful. This still involves ethical responsibility, but it often can be used for purposes of genuine encouragement. The responsibility of speakers is thus to identify all possible divisions and to avoid unnecessary or unintentional castigation of other groups, even in the name of the most noble and respectable goal or virtue. As history has shown, many of the greatest atrocities were committed by those who truly believed they were fighting in the name of truth and freedom and goodness. As important as it is to be motivated by noble values and inspiring identifications, it is also important to analyze who is being excluded or condemned.

Conclusion

Ethos is something given to a speaker by an audience based on how a speaker displays himself or herself within a particular rhetorical situation. In most of our everyday interactions, the Aristotelian categories of goodwill, practical wisdom, and virtue are usually sufficient for acquiring ethos. However, developing a message that also supports one's ethos requires further conceptual strategies. *Persona* provides a way of developing a specific presentation style that can balance the needs of a specific situation with the imperative to maintain consistency in character. An *evoked audience* amplifies certain qualities that are already shared by members of an audience and then given a concrete name and identity that serves as an appropriate response to a rhetorical situation. *Identification* acts as a natural bridge between persona and the evoked audience, as it represents a way of creating a common "we" out of an "I" and "you," even while retaining certain differences. *Distinction* takes for granted the assumption of identification but seeks to add extra qualities to make the speaker stand out from the group. Lastly, *polarization* occurs when a speaker attempts to further solidify the identification of a group by comparing its members with an outsider group that represents the opposite in values and goals. Some degree of polarization is virtually inevitable in any speech, but one must always be careful to reduce its possible negative impacts to a minimum. We can have goodwill, after all, even toward those who disagree with us or are unlike us.

Discussion Questions

1   Although we think of the three parts of Aristotelian ethos as always appearing together, rarely does a single person display virtue, practical wisdom, and goodwill all at once. In what types of situations might it not matter that a person is deficient in one?
2   Think of the typical encounters you have during the day. How many distinct personae do you tend to adopt when dealing with different people in different situations?
3   When we move to different places, change schools, or have major life changes, we often have the opportunity to invent an entirely new

persona. Have you ever experienced this in your life? When did you feel you became literally a "new" person?

4   We often underestimate the power of evoked audience. But often we look forward to the opportunity to step into a new role when we do so with others. When did you find yourself accepting an invitation like this even when you didn't expect it?

5   In an age of social media, the methods of identification have quite literally been incorporated into algorithms. We are invited to select our interests in order to network with like-minded others. Do you think this has increased individuality or fixed us into set patterns?

6   How are products today marketed using identification? What types of qualities are emphasized with certain products, for instance, alcohol versus smartphones versus cleaning products versus fashion?

7   Distinction tends to be a double-edged sword. We want to look to people for advice, at the same time that elitism or snobbishness is frowned upon. How do today's popular social influencers achieve distinction while still creating identification?

8   Particularly in politics, polarization is often decried as damaging to democracy. However, polarization is also seen as necessary to warn us from destructive habits and ideas. Do you think there is a difference between "good" and "bad" polarization?

Exercises

1   **Sales pitch**: Find some object currently in your possession. Create an impromptu solicitation speech in which you attempt to "sell" this commodity to the class by using the following strategies in order: evoked audience, identification, distinction, and polarization. In the process, also develop a unique persona for yourself that acts as if you are a well-known salesperson with a following.

2   **Morning meeting**: Imagine you are the manager of a franchise of some kind. Invent the name for that franchise and define its business. Now, write a short administrative speech that tries to get your employees excited for their workday by using evoked audience and identification that references the shared vision of the "ideal" employee to do a great job. Be specific in the kinds of qualities these employees have in common and give hypothetical examples.

3   **Roommate breakup:** Write a speech in which you are kicking out a hypothetically bad roommate from your apartment or house. In your speech, you are representing not only yourself but the other members of the residence. Hence, show identification with them. However, use polarization to show how the roommate failed to live up to these standards, which makes them a "kind" of person who doesn't belong there. Give specific examples.

References

Aristotle, *Rhetoric*, available at http://classics.mit.edu/Aristotle/rhetoric.1.i.html (accessed March 24, 2022).

Black, Edwin. "The Second Persona," in *Readings in Rhetorical Criticism*, ed. Carl R. Burgchardt (State College, PA: Strata Publishing Co., 1995).

Burke, Kenneth. *A Rhetoric of Motives* (Berkeley, CA: University of California Press, 1969).

Darsey, James. "Edwin Black and the First Persona," *Rhetoric & Public Affairs* 10, no. 3 (2007), 501–507.

Foster, David E. "Bush's Use of the Terrorism and 'Moral Values' Issues in His 2004 Presidential Campaign Rhetoric: An Instance of the Rhetorical Strategy of Polarization," *Ohio Communication Journal* 44 (2006), 33–60.

Harpine, William D. "Bryan's 'A Cross of Gold': The Rhetoric of Polarization at the 1896 Democratic Convention," *Quarterly Journal of Speech* 87, no. 3 (2001), 291–304.

King, Andrew and Floyd Douglas Anderson, "Nixon, Agnew, and the 'Silent Majority': A Case Study in the Rhetoric of Polarization," *Western Speech* 35, no. 4 (1971), 243–255.

McGee, Michael. "In Search of the People," *Quarterly Journal of Speech* 71 (1975), 235–249.

Wander, Philip. "The Third Persona: An Ideological Turn in Rhetorical Theory," *Central States Speech Journal* 35 (1984), 197–216.

Whitehead, Jack. "Factors of Source Credibility," *Quarterly Journal of Speech* 54 (1968), 59–63.

Woodward, Gary C. *The Idea of Identification* (Albany, NY: State University of New York Press, 2003).

8 Logos

The rhetorical character of *logos* was present at its very origin. When citizens of Classical Greece used the word *logos*, it referred to *words, arguments*, or *reason*. For example, the term *dissoi logoi* (meaning "double arguments") was a common phrase that referred to the Greek belief that there were always two or more arguments opposed on every issue. The Greeks acquired this belief largely because of their reliance on courts of law to decide almost any dispute. Any time two people came into conflict, their instinct was to bring this conflict into court in order to hear both sides and come to a practical judgment. In these sorts of rhetorical contexts, **logos** refers to the use of rational arguments and evidence to persuade an audience of the reasonableness of one's position. It is based on the belief that human beings are rational beings with the potential to make decisions based on logic, principles, and evidence.

The study of rhetoric corresponded with the study of logic, for both were grounded in the faith that human beings are rational creatures who seek reasons for their actions. Without the faith that people make better practical judgments when presented with more comprehensive and accurate facts, we would be forced to rely purely on either habit, passion, or luck. The difference between rhetoric and logic is that whereas logic examines the validity and coherence of argumentative propositions apart from the situated context of action, rhetoric is concerned with how arguments affect specific audiences in specific times and places. In addition, rhetoric does not neglect the importance of other rhetorical appeals like ethos and pathos. Rhetoricians understand that while reason plays a vital role in human decision making, it is rarely, if ever, sufficient for successful persuasion. Often, our emotions are necessary to judge right from wrong, effective from ineffective, and pleasure from pain. Likewise, our ability to discern who is a more reliable advisor during times of crisis can rarely be made by logic alone. In fact, our need to trust other people usually arises precisely when logic reaches its practical limit. The very idea of the rhetorical situation supports this conclusion—for if we had all the facts that we needed to make a decision, we would hardly need to be persuaded of anything.

In rhetoric, therefore, **logical reasoning** comes into play any time we use inferences, evidence and reasons to prove our points. Whenever we

DOI: 10.4324/9781003316787-8

debate with ourselves or with others about why one thing or action is better than another and use facts to defend or arrive at our conclusion, we engage in the process of logical reasoning. Put more simply, logical reasoning occurs any time we give a "reason why." A bare *assertion* ("It is sunny today"), *request* ("Let's get going"), or *definition* ("The best beach is one with the best waves") does not engage us in logical reasoning. Only when we provide a reason for these utterances do we start the process of making **inferences**, which is the act or process of deriving conclusions from premises known or assumed to be true. For instance, let us say I wake up and say "It is sunny today, because I see light coming through the window shades" or "Let's get going, because we don't want to get caught in traffic" or "The best beach is the one with the best waves, so let's go to the North Shore." In each of these arguments, we are drawing inferences to make these comprehensible.

A statement has the capacity to be "logical" only when it has the possibility to be refuted on its own terms. By "on its own terms," I mean apart from the ability to simply point to something objective as proof that the opposite is the case. If I say "It is sunny today" when it is actually raining, then you can simply point outside and say "No, it isn't." Then you have rejected this claim through empirical observation. But this is not a *logical* refutation showing an argument to be invalid; it is an *empirical* rejection showing a fact to be false. A logical refutation examines the reasoning as one might look at a mathematical formula, as a series of premises and conclusions. If I say "there are three donuts" and you see there are only two, that is an empirical rejection. But if I say "I have three donuts, and since there are four of us, each of us gets a donut," this claim can be refuted on its own terms. Quite simply, the conclusion does not follow from the premises any more than "3 divided by 4 equals 1." Of course, in any actual situation, rejecting a claim involves both logical and empirical argument. We are almost always concerned not only with logical coherence but also with empirical accuracy. But in rhetoric, it is the process of reasoning itself that is the focus of art.

Rhetorical Argumentation

The idea that rhetoric had a different style of argumentation than logic was one of Aristotle's core principles. For Aristotle, the essential instrument of logic was what he called the **syllogism** (*si* / luh / ji / zm). The syllogism represents a complete form of reasoning with all parts clearly defined and explicit, like a very clear mathematical formula. The most common example of a syllogism is as follows:

All human beings are mortal (*major premise*)
Socrates is a human being (*minor premise*)
Socrates is mortal (*conclusion*)

The syllogism allows us to organize our experience by fitting particular things into general categories, so we know what to expect of them. The **major premise** represents a general rule that describes what a category of things are like: for instance, that "all smartphones have cameras." The **minor premise** indicates in what category a particular thing belongs: "This phone is a smartphone." The **conclusion** then applies the rule of the major premise to describe the particular event, object, person, or action of the minor premise: "This phone has a camera." For Aristotle, the ideal syllogism possessed a rational and certain major premise, a factually observable minor premise, and a certain conclusion, with each step made explicit.

However, Aristotle also recognized that people in everyday life did not speak in this way. People relied on uncertain and vague principles and often spoke in short phrases that left out a good deal. For instance, if a person today wanted to take a picture, they might just say: "Can I borrow your phone? I need to take a selfie." Here, the speaker assumes an awareness that smartphones all come with cameras. Aristotle called this type of reasoning an **enthymeme** (*en* / thuh / meem), which was a form of argumentation, often based on probabilities, that strategically left out many of the premises in order to appeal to an audience. The idea was that, by allowing an audience to "fill in" or "supply" the premises on their own, it not only made communication quicker but also encouraged involvement. Take, for instance, the request, "put your phones away, I want to have a conversation." Before smartphones, this phrase would not make any sense, as a phone with a "land line" was precisely a tool for conversation. But today, this statement implies that people are using their smartphones as tablets and thus staring silently at the apps on their screens instead of talking to the people in front of them. Enthymemes are therefore arguments that rely on a certain amount of shared knowledge, values, and attitudes in an audience that can be relied upon to fill in the gaps.

A good public speaker should make argumentation look and feel "easy" to an audience. But this effect only is produced through a great deal of conscious labor beforehand. The art of the well-crafted argument is in identifying the parts of an argument that a particular audience already believes and is ready and willing to draw upon in filling out the logical assertion. As Aristotle emphasized, the most successful arguments are those in which the speaker gives the audience just enough for them to complete the argument on their own. Too much information makes a speech tiring and pedantic; too little information makes a speech obscure and confusing. But if the speaker can craft an argument that leaves out premises that the audience is ready and willing to contribute to the completion of the logical proposition, then audience members become active participants in the construction of meaning, which brings about a pleasurable feeling of learning without even realizing they are doing so.

There are six different types of logical reasoning to choose from when constructing effective arguments: *authority, principle, cause, sign, analogy,* and *generalization*. We will focus purely on how to construct an effective enthymeme that can potentially serve as one of the main points of a speech. Particularly when designing an advocacy speech, beginning each of the sections of your argument with a very clear and logical main point is essential to moving an audience step-by-step toward a reasoned practical judgment.

Authority

Arguments from **authority** justify an idea by the credibility, expertise, and status of the source of that idea. These types of argument do not rely on any other justification for reaching a conclusion. A speaker simply gives a statement legitimacy by attributing it to an authoritative source. The persuasive basis of these types of arguments therefore derives entirely from the preexisting trust that an audience possesses in that source. For instance, religious leaders constantly rely upon the authority of sacred texts to make moral assertions. Scientific researchers cite publications from respected peer-reviewed journals. Lawyers cite common law precedents in their arguments. Supreme Court justices cite the Constitution in their decisions. Politicians cite news stories from friendly-leaning news organizations. Arguments from authority are employed any time you are citing a respected source to justify your position. Appealing to authorities is like making allies; the more respected people you can have by your side or at your back, the stronger your position. These arguments take the generic forms: "Something is the case because this respected authority said so" or "According to this authority, this is the case." For instance: "According to the Surgeon General, smoking causes cancer."

Principle

Arguments by **principle** tell us what to do or to expect from something by appealing to widely shared maxims, definitions, and norms. These principles categorize whole classes of people, events, objects, and actions according to their shared properties and characteristics. A principle is defined as any rule ("always love your neighbor"), law ("all murderers go to prison"), doctrine ("all democracies are based on freedom"), or definition ("all cats are carnivores") that helps guide judgment in particular cases by classifying types of objects, events, or people. To argue by principle is thus to apply one of those statements to some particular thing that belongs to that classification. For instance, if I don't know how to behave toward the actual person who lives next to me, the rule "love your neighbor" would tell me what to do. If I didn't know what to feed my cat, the definition "all cats are carnivores" would inform me. In other words, principles organize and classify the particular things of this world according to general categories and classifications. Principles give order to complexity and use established definitions as guidelines for judgment and action. They take the generic forms: "Because this specific thing is also this general type of thing, this is what to expect of it" or "We should act this way because a rule has been established that we should always act this way in this type of situation." For instance, "Because this is rice cereal, it is gluten free" or "As I am a pacifist, I hate war."

Arguments from principle can be thought of as **deductive** forms of argument, meaning they begin with a rule and then deduce specific consequences or responsibilities from it. Accordingly, principles are the foundations of traditional moral action. Principles give us not only definitions to make sense of our world but give us a list of imperatives that, as certain types of people in certain circumstances, we should or should not do. Arguments by principle are particularly powerful when they inhabit this tension between the ideal and the actual in a way that motivates thought and action.

Generalization

Rhetors use arguments from **generalization** when they draw general conclusions from either a series of examples or a single powerful anecdote. Generalization therefore entails drawing a general conclusion about a class of people, events, objects, or processes based on specific examples drawn from experience. In other words, it is the opposite of argument by principle. Whereas principle uses deduction by beginning with a general rule and moving to a specific conclusion, generalization is an **inductive** argument because it begins with specific instances and using them to justify the creation of a general rule. Another way to define generalization is argument by example. When an argument by generalization is structured as a main point, this part of the speech usually focuses on providing one or a number of specific cases that are shown to be representative of a general state of affairs. Generalization uses these examples to prove that a general tendency or character exists. As a main point, generalization is useful to introduce a close analysis of specific instances, examples, statistics, or case studies to prove. Arguments by generalization take the generic forms: "These specific instances all show this general condition to be true" or "As this example shows, this generally is the case for all such examples." For instance, "I owned two cats and they both woke me up at night. So I think they all do that."

As indicated by these generic arguments, there is no set number of examples or instances that one must use. One might cite statistics that deal with thousands of specific instances to prove a general rule, such as an opinion poll that proves that most voters support some policy. Or one might select a smaller number of vivid examples to draw a conclusion, such as a narrative that describes how three different close relatives who smoked all had lung disease in their old age, thus proving that smoking is bad for everybody's health. Or one might even use a single, detailed representative example, such as the sampling of one taste of a wine as a way of judging the quality of the entire bottle or even the vintage. What allows the glass of wine to be representative, however, is that it was selected from a relatively uniform source. One could not make the same generalization in opinion polls by talking to a single individual because of the diversity of opinions in any population. Similarly, if a glass of wine were left out in the hot sun for a day, it would no longer be representative of the wine still in a cooled bottle. The challenge with making arguments from generalization is therefore to determine how reliably a single example can stand in for multiple examples and therefore justify a general conclusion.

Analogy

Arguments from **analogy** invite us to accept a claim by inviting us to treat something unfamiliar as we would treat something more familiar. An analogy warrants us to treat two essentially unlike things the same way because they share a vital similarity that is particularly relevant to the case at hand.[1] Like metaphor, what makes arguments from analogy persuasive is that they allow the audience to transfer the qualities from something very familiar to some other thing that might be unclear or confusing. For instance, to say that "love is a battlefield, so come armed," uses an analogy to help someone prepare for the challenges of a relationship. But analogy need not be as poetic as metaphor. One might draw on historical parallels, like efforts to gain perspective on the decline of a great power by making an analogy with the fall of the Roman Empire, or make comparisons between similar objects, like describing an unfamiliar food by comparing it to a more familiar one, such as the argument that if you like chicken, you'll like alligator.

As a main point, an argument by analogy introduces an extended analysis of the more familiar object of comparison that then is used to interpret the subject matter at issue. In other words, if you were to use the Roman Empire to highlight the problems of the contemporary United States, the bulk of the main point would concern the Roman Empire. Only after inviting an audience to understand the more familiar object do you then turn to the more complicated topic. It is therefore important not to be in haste. Take time with an analogy to make it work. They take the generic forms: "Like this familiar thing, we can expect the same qualities of this unfamiliar thing" or "We can treat this thing as we treat this other thing." For instance, "Like the fascist regimes of the twentieth century, that country is descending into authoritarianism."

Sign

Arguments from **sign** use external cues, symptoms, characteristics, or qualities to discern the identity of someone or to diagnose some state of affairs. In other

1   For more on argument by analogy, see James R. Wilcox and Henry L. Ewbank, "Analogy for Rhetors," *Philosophy and Rhetoric* 12 (1979), 1–20; James S. Measell, "Classical Bases of the Concept of Analogy," *Argumentation and Advocacy* 10 (1973), 1–10.

words, a sign defines what we cannot see by what we can see. It asks us to accept a state of affairs by careful reading of external clues or indicators. Arguments based on sign are usually called for in situations when people are concerned with identifying what is going on, what is present, or what condition something is in. If we are lost, for instance, we might literally look for signs to tell us where we are. If we are sick, we go to the doctor to diagnose our symptoms to discern the underlying cause. If we meet a stranger, we look for signs in their clothes, demeanor, or language to determine their identity. Naturally, arguments from signs are most commonly used either in forensic argumentation that deals with proving the guilt or innocence of a person based on what evidence shows the individual has done in the past, or in deliberative policy discussions that require us to diagnose the present situation by the reading of present indicators. In almost all popular crime shows, there are scenes in which investigators walk onto the scene of a crime and read signs ordinarily gone unnoticed that reveal some important aspects of what happened and who committed the crime. But forensic investigation also deals with how we determine whether or not a lake is polluted, or whether the economy is growing, or whether some foreign power is preparing for war. All of these arguments tell us "what is the case" based on a gathering together of clues and evidence and facts that point to a specific conclusion.

Arguments from sign usually come in one of two forms. In the first case, the argument is that a certain event happened in a certain way based on available evidence. For instance, the prosecution in a court trial might argue: "because the bloodstain on the knife matched that of the victim, this knife was the murder weapon." Here we have a specific sign (the blood on the knife) pointing to a state of affairs (that the knife was the murder weapon). The second type of argument by sign declares the identity of something based on visible signs. For instance, if I am looking for help in a store, I might go up to someone and ask: "I see from your name badge that you work here, can I ask you a question?" Here we have a specific sign (the name badge) pointing to an identity (that the person is an employee). We can then use the same reasoning for larger issues. Environmental signs might indicate rapid climate change, a military buildup might indicate an intention to go to war, a rise in depression in young people might indicate overuse of social media, the gentrification of neighborhoods might indicate the rising wealth of a city. Arguments from sign take on the generic forms: "As we see from this tangible sign, this underlying condition is present" or "This person or object belongs to this class as proven by its possession of these tangible qualities or characteristics" or "These present pieces of evidence show that this thing had happened or will happen."

Causation

We use **causal** arguments to predict what will happen or explain why something happened based on a relationship between cause and effect.

Arguments from causation assert that certain consequences or effects will naturally follow some specific interaction of elements in a situation. In other words, cause tells us why an effect came about in the past or predicts what we might expect in the future if certain causes are in place. Unlike sign, which diagnoses the presence or identify of something, cause focuses on those elements which change. Reading the signs might help a doctor diagnose the presence of an infection, but the prescription of antibiotics is based on causal reasoning that it will bring about the effect of a cure. Also, cause is different from principle in significant ways. Principle tells us that all things that belong in a certain category have a specific property, as in "all carrots contain vitamin A." Cause tells us that when two things interact, one thing will bring about changes in the other, such as in "you should eat carrots to maintain good eye health." Cause brings together carrots and eyes and shows how one influences the other. Arguments from cause take the generic form: "This effect has been brought about by this cause" or "We should stop or start doing this action because it causes this effect" or "If we want to bring about this effect, we need to embrace this cause." For instance, "If you don't want to get cancer, stop smoking" or "More exercise will help you lose weight."

Main points that are structured as arguments from cause are therefore almost always focused on documenting the effects that are desirable or undesirable from the presence of something or the implementation of some policy. As a result, they typically use the words "if" and "because," as in "*if* we wish to avoid global warming, we must reduce greenhouse gases" or "*because* of the burning of fossil fuels, the levels of carbon dioxide have dramatically increased over the last century." Hence, as in the example above, one argument might diagnose the underlying cause of a problem, and a second causal argument will justify an action based on a prediction of a positive effect. If a single main point combined these two types of arguments into one claim, it might be "Because fossil fuels have risen carbon dioxide levels so high in the past century, we need to dramatically cut emissions to control global warming." Causal arguments to be effective must then be sure to prove the causal relationship through careful scientific, historical, or moral reasoning, often relying also on arguments by respected authorities.

Fallacies

A fallacy is an error in logical reasoning. There are two perspectives from which an argument can be considered a fallacy. From a purely logical standpoint, a fallacy occurs when the conclusion does not follow from the major and minor premises. In other words, logical fallacies are determined by analyzing an argument "on its own terms." For instance, it would be faulty reasoning to say that "since it is dangerous outside, we better leave the house to be safe." From a practical rhetorical standpoint, a fallacy occurs when an argument so clearly violates common sense that any reasonable person would find it incorrect. A rhetorical standpoint allows factual and practical aspects to be used to evaluate an argument. For instance, it would violate common sense to say "all Mondays are terrible because this Monday I had a really bad day." Because it is common sense that every day is different for every person, nobody would accept that a single experience on a single day allows a person to generalize about the condition of every day.

Fallacies, therefore, are not simply untrue or unreliable arguments. A person can simply be incorrect without committing a fallacy. An argument is not a fallacy, in other words, if under certain reasonable conditions it might be true. For instance, there is nothing unreasonable about the statement: "If you want to get some onions, go to the supermarket right now." Everybody knows that a supermarket is a place to buy onions. If that statement were made at 3 a.m. in the morning when all the stores are closed, it would be bad advice, but it would not be a fallacy. However, a statement would be a fallacy if it said: "We don't need to buy any onions, so go to the supermarket to buy one." This statement, at least taken literally, would be a fallacy at any time because it doesn't make any sense on its own terms.

Unfortunately, fallacies are common in rhetoric because, despite being illogical, they are often effective as means of persuasion. Especially when speaking to an audience who is already predisposed to agree with the speaker's position, fallacies often serve to flatter, surprise, and delight an audience. Precisely because they violate standards of reasoning, they can often appear bold and shocking. However, especially at a time when speeches are recorded and often can have a long afterlife on the internet, a fallacy that pleases the crowd in the moment can lead to embarrassment when time has passed. A responsible speaker should thus be careful to avoid fallacies and compose arguments that can hold up over time. The following are common fallacies.

Hasty Overgeneralization

We are often quick to judge entire classes of people and objects based on single experiences. A **hasty overgeneralization** makes broad assumptions about things based on trivial or unreliable instances, usually because the conclusions flatter our own biases. It argues: "Everything of this type is just like this one thing." For instance, a person who just had a bad breakup might say: "I learned from this experience that all relationships are poisonous." Sometimes, we are tempted to make overgeneralizations when we encounter single cases that are so vivid and powerful that they capture our imagination and our emotions in a way that distorts our judgment. Other times, we make overgeneralizations because they simplify the world and take away the responsibility for judging individuals on their own merits. Perhaps the most common form of hasty overgeneralization is **stereotyping**, which treats a diverse group of people as if they all were the same, thereby reducing a complex population to a simple and monolithic entity.

Post Hoc

This fallacy is also known simply as **false cause**, which attributes an effect to something which has no actual causal connection. But post hoc is a specific type of false cause which gets its name from the Latin phrase "post hoc, ergo propter hoc," which translates as "after this, therefore because of this." In other words, **post hoc** falsely reasons that just because two things followed each other in sequence, that the first thing must have caused the second thing. It argues: "This thing happened first, so it must have brought about the second thing." For instance, "The President passed a law raising gas taxes, and the next day we had a terrorist attack. Coincidence? I don't think so." These types of arguments usually border on superstition. But they are common because they provide an easy connection to praise or blame actions that simply happened together. Consequently, they are usually the first fallacies to be used whenever people are trying to score easy points by taking credit for doing something they did not or blaming someone for something for which they weren't responsible.

Slippery Slope

Whenever someone wants to prohibit any and all actions that point in a certain direction, the slippery slope fallacy comes to the rescue. The **slippery slope** fallacy takes the form of an argument that claims we must not make an even incremental step in a certain direction if we are to prevent a dramatic slide and decline into a terrible state of affairs. It argues: "If we do this one small thing, a chain of ever larger and worse things will inevitably happen in sequence." The logic of the slippery slope is fatalistic. It argues that once a chain reaction begins, it cannot be stopped or redirected. One ends on a "slippery slope," like an icy hill, that forces us to go straight to the bottom. And the bottom is always a bad and disastrous thing in this fallacy. For instance, "If we decriminalize marijuana, soon we are going to have heroin dealers on every street corner." Slippery slope relies on hyperbole but does so as if the exaggeration were true. It therefore relies on paranoia and fear to make people scared of trying something new.

Weak Analogy

Although analogies are very useful in helping understand unfamiliar things through comparison with familiar ones, they also can easily be misleading. A **weak analogy** makes logically absurd or ethically dubious associations between two things that have very little relationship to one another in order to distort the reality of the situation. It argues: "These two things share some trivial quality, so they share all qualities." Weak analogies are usually made when the desired effect is either to fear or desire something. For instance, "A machine gun and a baseball bat can both kill people, but you don't see people banning baseball bats." Or, "I am against war in all forms, that's why I don't let my kids play sports." In both cases, one begins with a superficial connection between two things—that both items can be used as weapons, or that both activities involve competition. But then the argument goes far beyond any sense of proportion to make a point.

Appeal to Authority

Although arguments from authority are important for establishing credibility and citing important facts, they can easily drift into the realm of fallacy when not constructed responsibly. As a fallacy, an **appeal to authority** suggests that people should accept an idea simply because it was expressed by a charismatic individual not because he or she has any particular expertise in the subject, but because that individual is liked by the audience. It argues: "You should believe this idea because this well-liked person said it." For instance, "We should be suspicious of vaccines because this popular actress on an old 1980s sitcom said they were dangerous." Unfortunately, appeals to authority are very common in an age of digital social influencing. Many people today get much of their information not from traditional sources but from informal posts on social media by people who have developed large followings. Appeals to authority tend to think first of popularity first without tracing the idea back to its original source.

Ad Populum

Similar to appeal to authority, the *ad populum* fallacy uses popularity as a way of evaluating worth and credibility. The Latin name of this fallacy means "to the people," indicating that it is to the people that one should look for guidance. Also known as the **bandwagon** fallacy, *ad populum* asks an audience to jump on board an idea because everybody else is already riding the wagon. It argues: "A lot of people like or do not like this thing, so you should too." For instance, "This fast food restaurant serves the best food because there is a restaurant in every city." But *ad populum* does not always need to be about the majority. It can also be used within smaller groups or subcultures that share certain beliefs. For instance, "there are so many flat-earthers out there that they can't be wrong." Once again, *ad populum* fallacies are very tempting in an Internet age when anything can be quantified or subject to an instant poll. Whenever we encounter a new or unfamiliar object or idea, we are tempted to simply follow the majority as a guide for our own beliefs and attitudes. To be sure, often following the crowd can be practically useful. But the fallacy makes a stronger case that popularity is also a sign of accuracy, morality, and truth.

Appeal to Ignorance

Often tied with both *ad populum* and appeal to authority is the **appeal to ignorance**, which argues that because there appears to be neither conclusive evidence nor consensus among experts about an issue, then any view is equally plausible and should be considered. It argues: "Since nobody knows for sure, this completely unverified opinion should be adopted." For instance, "because evolutionary theorists still haven't found the missing link between primates and humans, then the theory of divine creation should be taught in schools alongside evolution." This appeal is tied with these other fallacies because it is often used by popular spokespeople to promote highly suspect theories amongst people eager for something new and different. Appeal to ignorance opens the door to all manner of explanations about mysterious phenomena and is common in conspiracy theories.

Appeal to Pity

Although emotional appeals are important to help focus attention and energy on an issue, it can also be used to distort our judgment. The **appeal to pity** happens when a speaker invites people to accept a person's conclusion by making them feel sorry for that person or group. It argues: "This person is suffering and has been victimized, therefore he or she is also correct." For instance, "these people are out of work and can't pay their mortgage, and they believe it is the new immigrants who took their jobs." Our natural human impulse to sympathize with suffering, particularly with people with whom we identify, can easily lead us to desire to agree with them. Emotional appeal should never be used to short-circuit our rational process, but it is very tempting to give in to pity under conditions of high stress and visible suffering.

Scapegoating

Because it can be so easily combined with other fallacies, one of the most common forms of fallacious reasoning is **scapegoating,** which places blame for some problem on a particular group of people that the audience already doesn't like. It argues: "This undesirable thing is caused by these people." For instance, during the Salem witch trials, a series of hardships, including disease and famine, were blamed on "witches" mostly in the form of women on the outskirts of society. Scapegoating is often combined with post hoc, appeal to authority, *ad populum*, and appeal to pity, among others. Any time some "out group" is mentioned in connection with negative effects, scapegoating is almost always implied even when it is not made explicit. The speaker usually can rely on the biases of an audience to connect the dots.

Ad Hominem

Like the appeal to authority and *ad populum* fallacies, the *ad hominem* (in Latin, "against the person") focuses not on the quality of the argument from the character of a person or group. **Ad hominem** makes the claim that because a speaker has questionable character, then the audience should immediately dismiss that person's argument without question. In other words, in an *ad hominem* argument, the arguer attacks his or her opponent instead of the opponent's argument. It argues: "This person is wrong because he or she is not a good person." For instance, "Why should we take economic advice from a man who is three times married?" Particularly in an internet age when everyone's flaws can be easily exposed and exaggerated, there is always an opportunity to use *ad hominem* to dismiss our opponent's arguments without having to put in the effort to understand them. Character does matter, to be sure, but it should not be used as an excuse to reject arguments out of hand.

Straw Man

One variation of *ad hominem* is to combine it with the straw man fallacy, whose name comes from the notion that one can construct an artificial person out of straw for the purposes of destroying it. Specifically, to argue with a **straw man** is to put a simplistic, false, and offensive position in the mouth of one's opponents for the purpose of rejecting that argument and humiliating one's opponent. It argues: "My opponents are saying these ridiculous things that violate everything we hold dear, so why should we listen to them?" For instance, "Those who want socialized medicine want to tell you how to live and when to die." A straw man plays to the fears and biases of an audience, and attributes to one's opponent every value and belief that the audience finds offensive. This allows a speaker to appear to be reasoning from both sides, when in fact they are only presenting one perspective.

Red Herring

Another way of distracting an audience from a careful consideration of an issue is to get them off the track entirely. The red herring fallacy derives from a story where a person used a strong-smelling smoked fish to turn pursuing hounds off the track of a rabbit. Similarly, the **red herring** fallacy uses a provocative side-issue to distract an audience from the main subject so that they concentrate on an unrelated, but emotionally powerful, matter instead. Usually, the speaker never returns to the main topic. It argues: "The main issue is this, and to better understand it, we should concentrate on this completely irrelevant but more flashy side-issue." For instance, "We are confronted with the question of what to do about inflation, and right at this moment we see a rise in access to abortion!" Red herring thus uses an emotionally charged subject to turn an audience away from the more important, but also more complicated, main subject. And as audiences sometimes want to be entertained and flattered more than informed, they willingly follow along because the trip is pleasurable.

Either/Or

Yet another way of over-simplifying the problem is to eliminate any complex, overlapping, or "fuzzy" middle ground. The **either/or** fallacy polarizes two alternatives and makes them appear as if they were irreconcilable opposites. Typically, this fallacy makes one alternative seem morally abhorrent and practically disastrous (using a straw man fallacy) while the other appear virtuous and prudent (using the *ad populum* fallacy). This fallacy comes to an erroneous conclusion that if anything does not belong to one category, that it must be the exact opposite. It argues: "There are one two paths, and you must choose either one or the other." For instance, "We are at war with terrorists, so you are either with us or against us." Either/or framing of issues is extremely common in partisan and sectarian conflicts because they force people into a corner. Because there is no middle ground, a person must say "yes" or "no." Once a person admits a "yes," they are therefore committed to a course of action or a system of beliefs they didn't initially intend.

Conclusion

In rhetoric, logos is the art of crafting one's arguments to make those reasons persuasive. Perhaps the most important aspect of this art is to know what to leave out. More often than not, amateur speakers put in too much rather than too little. They pile arguments on top of arguments as if persuasion occurred by the sheer weight of argumentation. However, a good speech will actually include only a few actual arguments, with each argument in effect representing a main point. The rest of the speech will then focus on providing backing for those arguments in various ways, including resources from ethos, pathos, and style. The art of crafting arguments is to therefore appeal to those premises that the audience already believes and are eager to use to help a speaker establish his or her claims. This means that a good argument from logos begins with an understanding of the audience, proceeds to making explicit the premises that they will readily assent to, and then finally to building arguments that invoke those premises without needing to verbalize them.

One way to explain this process is through the Aristotelian-inspired model developed by Stephen Toulmin.[2] It is Toulmin that redefined

---

2   This model is elaborated in Stephen Toulmin, *The Uses of Argument* (Cambridge: Cambridge University Press, 1958). See also Wayne Brockriede and Douglas Ehninger, "Toulmin on Argument: An Interpretation and Application," *Quarterly Journal of Speech* 46 (1960), 44–53.

Aristotle's major premise, minor premise, and conclusion as warrant, grounds, and claim. A **claim** is the primary position or conclusion being advanced by a speaker that represents the "payoff" of the reasoning ("We should drink more red wine."). The **grounds** are the supporting evidence for the claim that represents the "proof" for the conclusion ("Because we want to savor the good life."). The **warrant** is the inferential leap that connects the claim with the ground, usually embodied in a principle, provision, or chain of reasoning ("Wine is a necessary condition for bringing about the good life."). What makes this relationship subtle is the fact that the warrant is often (but not always) left unstated because more often than not it is taken for granted. Except in very complex chains of reasoning, we usually assume that audience members will "fill in" warrants for themselves by drawing from their own resources of common sense, experience, and education. For instance, if we say "you should drink some water, because you are probably thirsty," we leave out the warrant "water quenches thirst" because it is obvious. But invoke an absurd or false warrant and it immediately becomes obvious to us. If I said "you should drink some whiskey, because you are probably thirsty," we would probably laugh because nobody drinks whiskey for quenching thirst. That is what makes it funny.

There are six types of warrants that are used in logical argumentation: *authority, principle, causal, sign, analogy*, and *generalization*. An **authority** warrant justifies accepting a claim because of the credibility of its source: for instance, "trust what this doctor says." A **principle** warrant defines an entire class of things by associating them with a specific property: for instance, "All candy is sweet." A **causal** warrant explains that the presence of a class of objects/activities/events will bring about a specific effect: for instance, "Eating a lot of candy will make you gain weight." A **sign** warrant declares that certain sensible properties are indicative of the presence of a certain class of objects: for instance, "A funny aftertaste means that something is sugar-free candy." An **analogy** warrant suggests that a less familiar object or class of objects can be treated the same way as a more familiar object or class of objects: for instance, "We can treat chocolate mousse like we treat chocolate pudding.". A **generalization** warrant licenses us to treat an entire class of objects in the same way that we treat a specific individual case or selection of individual cases: for instance, "All candy from this bag is sweet because this one piece of candy from the bag was sweet." All warrants thus follow these general patterns. If a warrant cannot be rephrased in one of these ways, it is probably not a warrant but a claim or a ground. Here are some other examples stated as syllogisms. (To make them enthymemes, simply remove one of the claims and rearrange the order or presentation):

- Principle

  Warrant:"All intentional killing is murder."
  Grounds:"Capital punishment is an intentional killing."
  Claim:"Capital punishment is murder."

- Causal

  Warrant:"Smoking causes cancer."
  Grounds:"You smoke."
  Claim:"You are going to get cancer."

- Sign

  Warrant:"A high fever is indicative of the flu."
  Grounds:"You have a high fever."
  Claim:"You have the flu."

- Analogy

  Warrant:"We can treat the Iraq War like the Vietnam War."
  Grounds:"The Vietnam War was a disaster."
  Claim:"The Iraq War will be a disaster."

- Generalization

  Warrant:"The behavior of my one cat is representative of the behavior of all cats."
  Grounds:"My cat always wakes me up at 3 a.m."
  Claim:"All cats wake you up at 3 a.m."

- Authority

  Warrant:"My accountant is always right about taxes."
  Grounds:"My accountant said to invest in technology stocks."
  Claim:"It's a good idea to invest in technology stocks."

One should think of arguments from logos as establishing an initial bond between speaker and audience in which the speaker provides a framework that the audience completes by filling in the missing warrant. This generates a sense of participation that does not have the same effect as when the speaker spells out every single part of an argument. By leaving essential aspects out that the audience can contribute on their own, it makes them more willing to consider the subsequent backing for that claim that constitutes the rest of the speech. The art of the well-crafted argument is in identifying the parts of an argument that a particular audience already believes and is ready and willing to draw upon in filling out the logical assertion. As Aristotle emphasized, the most successful arguments are those in which the speaker gives the audience just enough for them to complete the argument on their own. Too much information makes a speech tiring and pedantic; too little information makes a speech obscure and confusing. But if the speaker can craft an argument that uses warrants that the audience is ready and willing to contribute to the completion of the logical proposition, then audience members become active participants in the construction of meaning, which brings about a pleasurable feeling of learning without even realizing they are doing so.

Let us take, for example, a speaker who is advocating for universal health care and is speaking to a variety of different audiences. The warrants are thus chosen to appeal to the beliefs of the audience in order to construct a persuasive argument:

1   First, she speaks to a group of college graduates who she knows are anxious about being on their own. She makes the argument: "Without universal health care we are all at risk, as we have seen in the story of one student who was forced to abandon her long-term career goals because of the debt incurred by the injuries caused by an uninsured motorist," invoking the unstated warrant from *generalization*: "This recent graduate represents the possible fate of all recent graduates."

2   Second, she speaks to a group of economists who are mostly concerned about the effect of universal health care on long-term economic growth. She makes the argument: "We are headed down an economic spiral without health care, as we have seen from the rise in personal debt and bankruptcy caused by health costs," invoking the unstated warrant from *sign*: "Increased debt and bankruptcy are signs of future economic decline."

3   Third, she speaks to the executives of multinational corporations familiar with different forms of health care across the globe. She makes the argument: "The American system needs to move to a single-payer system because of the success we have seen in European nations," invoking the unstated warrant from *analogy*: "We can treat the American health care system like we treat the European health care system."

4   Fourth, she speaks to a group of working parents concerned about both costs and securing the future of their children's health. She makes the argument: "Universal health care is absolutely necessary if we are to avoid condemning our children to a life of poverty simply because they had the bad fortune to get sick while looking for a job," invoking the unstated warrant from *cause*: "Universal health care will help keep children out of poverty."

5   Fifth, she speaks to a group of constitutional scholars familiar and makes the argument: "We cannot shirk our responsibilities to cover those who become sick because that is a violation of the right to life that we see guaranteed by the Declaration of Independence," invoking the unstated *principle* that "all human beings should be guaranteed the right to life" that is promised the source of *authority* from the Declaration.

In each of these cases, the warrant acts either as a "bridge" between the claim and the grounds that explains why the two should appear together or as a "guide" that tells an audience that if you have one thing, another thing will naturally follow as a consequence. In short, all forms of reasoning help but go beyond what is immediately present before our eyes or our mind in order to make connections that expand our horizons of understanding.

When inventing arguments, then, *first* think about the perspective of your audience and consider what types of beliefs, attitudes, values, and shared experiences they possess. *Second*, think about which of these resources can be phrased as a logical proposition in the form of a warrant. *Third*, select from these warrants the ones you think are most relevant to your case and can be embedded within an argument. *Last*, carefully pair claims with grounds that "call forth" these warrants without having to state them explicitly. This process of thinking *with* the audience is the most essential step in creating a cooperative rather than an antagonistic relationship. Logic, in other words, is first and foremost an *ethical* practice when it comes to rhetoric, for it requires us to think first of others before we speak to them about their fears, desires, and interests.

Discussion Questions

1   Logical reasoning is often relied upon in jokes and puns. For instance, "a man walked into a bar (grounds) – he said 'ouch' (the claim)," thus invoking the causal warrant "walking into a hard metal object causes pain" instead of the expected warrant concerning what happens when one walks into a place that sells alcohol. What other jokes can you think of that rely on unspoken warrants for their humor?

2   Find a trending Tweet by some celebrity or public figure. Now analyze it according to logical reasoning. How many different arguments does it contain? Can you identify them all and reconstruct them using the Toulmin model?

3   Think about myths that often focus on the actions of single individuals or groups associated with the founding of any nation, city, or even university or corporation. How do these single examples operate by the logic of generalization to represent larger social groups or institutions? Is this way of generalizing fair?

4   Think of a recent pharmaceutical advertisement that markets some new pill for treating an important condition. How do they use sign and causal arguments in cooperation to diagnose the problem and advocate for a solution? And how is this dramatized in the visual components of the commercial?

5   Sports announcers often use colorful analogies when describing the actions of athletes. What types of analogies are popular in different types of sports? Why do you think analogies are so important to make the games interesting?

6   As children, we are often taught basic, general principles by our parents to help us navigate the world. Can you remember any of these general principles that you learned that, as you grew older, you realized grossly oversimplified a complex phenomenon?

7   Authority is complicated, because it is both a legitimate form of reasoning and a fallacy. What do you think is a responsible and irresponsible way to use the appeal to authority?

8   Fallacies are notoriously misleading and yet they are ever present and popular in our political discourse. Do you think fallacies ever have a role to play in politics? If you knew that using a fallacy might help support a "good" cause, would you use it?

Exercises

1   **Study habits**: In order to experiment with how arguments can build on one another, write an argument that diagnoses a cause of poor study habits that leads to bad grades. First, use argument by sign to establish the existence of bad study habits. Second, use argument by cause that identifies one cause (by pointing to something tangible) that produces these bad study habits. Third, use argument by generalization to give a specific example that shows why all such problems should be treated the same way. Fourth, use an argument from authority to show what we should do about the problem based on expertise. Fifth, use an argument by principle that refers to some maxim in order to prove our moral responsibility to deal with this problem. Lastly, use argument by analogy to give us a positive image of what will happen if we do the right thing.

2   **Blame game:** Imagine you have failed all your courses in a semester (or some other related failure). Now you have to account for this failure to your parents or some other responsible party. Make explicit use of four different fallacies that explains your failure by placing the blame elsewhere or distracting from the issue. Afterwards, identify which fallacies were the most persuasive.

3   **Food fight:** Break into groups and have each group select a different type of diet or food that they will defend as superior to other foods. Construct arguments justifying this choice using at least three different types of warrants. If time allows, after each group gives their speech, regroup and compose a follow-up argument that criticizes other groups and defends one's own position.

References

Brockriede, Wayne and Douglas Ehninger, "Toulmin on Argument: An Interpretation and Application," *Quarterly Journal of Speech* 46 (1960), 44–53.
Measell, James S. "Classical Bases of the Concept of Analogy," *Argumentation and Advocacy* 10 (1973): 1–10.
Toulmin, Stephen. *The Uses of Argument* (Cambridge: Cambridge University Press, 1958).
Wilcox, James R. and Henry L. Ewbank, "Analogy for Rhetors," *Philosophy and Rhetoric* 12 (1979): 1–20.

9 Pathos

In the Greek rhetorical tradition, **pathos** refers to the use of emotional appeals to persuade an audience. Whereas *ethos* persuades by the character and *logos* persuades by reasoning, *pathos* persuades by producing an emotional response in an audience that makes it favorable to one thing and/or unfavorable to another. The essence of pathos is vivid description, not logical exposition. Whenever one gives formal reasons, detailed accounts, or logical analysis, one is using logos; the appeal of logos is to one's cognitive belief structure based in propositions and facts. Pathos, by contrast, gives "life" to those beliefs. For example, a speaker can use logos to give a formal cost–benefit analysis for why addressing poverty helps people's lives at the same time that it improves the economy and cuts crime. But one can also describe the squalor of living in a slum, the diseases that beset a hungry child, the lost potential of dying addicts, and the success story of a person who discovered their inner potential through the help of a teacher. Pathos thus incorporates elements of narrative and style to sculpt powerful images that live in people's imaginations and make them *feel* ideas that logic can only *explain*. The best rhetoric, then, will always balance the use of pathos with a more reasonable logical analysis. There is nothing wrong with exaggeration when it is done for the purposes of getting an audience engaged and enthusiastic about an issue that it may have otherwise thought important. One must simply supplement this enthusiasm with the kind of practical judgment that can be produced only through long and careful forethought and analysis.[1]

Fortunately, a good narrative can easily combine reason and emotion in such a way to reconcile the tension between logos and pathos. As many of the examples used in this book have shown, public speakers rarely restrict themselves to making explicit claims that are grounded in empirical data and warranted by logical reasoning. More often than not, their claims are embedded in narrative stories. These stories may be personal, moral, historical, fictional, or demonstrative, but *as stories* they all share in a common

---

1   For the relationship between reason and emotion, see John M. Cooper, *Reason and Emotion: Essays on Ancient Moral Psychology and Ethical Theory* (Princeton, NJ: Princeton University Press, 1999).

DOI: 10.4324/9781003316787-9

aim, which is to give meaning to ideas by showing how they function over time in people's lives and in the environment in a way that is both pleasing as a story and plausible as an account. By presenting an argument in a form of a story that accurately represents reality in a coherent, engaging, and powerful manner, a speaker invites an audience to vicariously participate in a new vision of reality. The narratives we tell of our common histories have particular power in structuring our social organizations, our self-conceptions, and our relationships with other groups.

Understanding Emotions

Before looking more closely at how to structure an emotional narrative, it is important to understand the reason why emotions themselves have an inherently narrative structure. In his *Rhetoric*, Aristotle offers a definition of emotions (*pathē*) that remains an important resource for understanding their function in rhetoric. He writes that "the emotions are those things through which, by undergoing change, people come to differ in their judgments and what are accompanied by pain and pleasure, for example, anger, pity, fear, and other such things and their opposites."[2] Already, we see narrative elements in this definition. Narrative, after all, is first and foremost a story of how something changes over a temporal series of events. And second, a good narrative always includes aspects like success and defeat, rise and fall, and loss and gain, all of which convey some aspects of pleasure and pain. Aristotle then explains that to understand someone's emotions, we need to know three things: (a) that person's state of mind (i.e., "angry"); (b) the people, objects, events, or actions that produce the state of mind (i.e., "my roommate and the dirty dishes"); and (c) the reasons he or she feels this way (i.e., "I told him to clean up before my parents arrived and instead he made an even bigger pile"). Once again, the only way to relate all three of these things together is through a single, coherent narrative account. Once a rhetorician knows why a person was angry in the past, he or she can produce a narrative that would produce an angry response in an audience in the present that leads to action in the future. In Aristotle's treatise, he offers a definition of the following emotions (I have paraphrased these definitions based on Aristotle's ideas):

Anger	An impulse to inflict punishment on a specific individual in response to the pain of a conscious, obvious, unjustified slight with respect to oneself or one's friends and which is accompanied by the pleasure of imagining revenge.
Mildness	The pleasurable settling down and quieting of anger due to the elimination of the perceived threat or the subordination of one's enemy.

2   Aristotle, *On Rhetoric: A Theory of Civic Discourse*, trans. George Kennedy (Oxford: Oxford University Press, 1991), 1378a.

Love	Wishing good things for a person you consider to be good, and wishing them for the other person's own sake and not your own, accompanied by the pleasure in imagining their happiness.
Hate	To despise and wish evil upon a general class or group that one does not like and wishes to eliminate, accompanied by pain at knowing they exist and pleasure at wishing their elimination. Hate is unlike anger because whereas anger is excited by offenses that concern an individual and a specific slight, hate is directed at a category of things and is more difficult to remedy.
Fear	A pain or disturbance arising from a mental image of impending evil of a painful or destructive sort that one believes might actually occur in the near future.
Confidence	The pleasure of anticipation of future things conducive to safety because one imagines them near at hand and allowing one to act freely and without fear.
Shame	A pain or disturbance regarding that class of evils, in the present, past, or future, which we think will tend to our discredit and which are judged as evil in comparison with some established norm or principle.
Shamelessness	A certain contempt or indifference regarding the acts which bring about shame in the pleasure that accompanies willful rejection of virtue.
Benevolence	The pleasure in imagining oneself performing disinterested kindness in doing or returning good to another or to all others.
Pity	A sense of pain at what we take to be an evil of a destructive or painful kind, which befalls one who does not deserve it; and which we think we or our loved ones might be susceptible to in similar circumstances.
Indignation	A pain at the sight of undeserved good fortune due to the fact that such fortune could have been bestowed upon a more worthy individual.
Envy	A disturbing pain directed at the good fortune of an equal, felt not because one desires something, but because the other persons have it.
Emulation	A pain at what we take to be the presence, in the case. of persons who are by nature like us, of goods that are desirable and are possible for us to attain, accompanied by the pleasure of anticipating that one can possess them.
Contempt	The antithesis of emulation, a feeling by those in a position to be emulated to feel pleasure at one's own superiority and a painful disregard or disgust for those who do not possess the virtues or goods because of their perceived unworthiness.

Although Aristotle believed that in an ideal world, logos should reign supreme, he recognized in the actual world that emotional appeal is an inevitable and necessary part of any persuasive act. Aristotle's careful study of emotions, which occupied over a third of his book, showed the importance he placed upon it as a form of proof, despite his own misgivings about its use. Although people's emotions can certainly be manipulated for irrational ends, it is widely accepted today that the use of emotion in persuasion is no more or less ethical than the use of credibility or logic. This is because, far from "distorting" our judgments, emotions are what make judgments possible by giving us the motive to prefer one thing over another. Without emotional involvement in our surroundings, all the reason and credibility in the world would not encourage us to expend the least bit of energy to accomplish a task. That is why people who are "apathetic" (or "without pathos") are those who have an incapacity to make a judgment.

To better grasp the nature of emotion, we can place it in contrast to both a feeling and a mood. A **feeling** is an immediate sensory response to some environmental stimulation or physical state. Feelings make up the substance of our perceptual world and represent the basic elements that physically connect us with the world around us. For instance, hot and cold, bright and dark, bitter and sweet, rough and smooth, and loud and soft are all feelings. They may have emotional connotations, but as feelings they are simply sense impressions. Feelings are often used in tropes and schemes to give a speech a vivid appeal. In contradistinction, a **mood** is a completely general, non-objective, and pervasive quality of a person's personality that affects his or her judgments in all situational contexts, regardless of what is present. For instance, a person in a depressed mood experiences the same objects or events very differently than a person who feels cheerful. Moods are "non-objective" because they are not responses to the specific things in one's environment. Moods express themselves from the inside-out, whereas feelings come from the outside-in. Changing one's mood can thus often be a long and difficult process.[3]

Emotions are something in between a feeling and a mood. Like a feeling, an emotion is a response to specific aspects of our world. Emotions are objective and respond to things outside of us. But like moods, emotions invest these objects with qualities that relate to our own attitudes. Emotions interpret feelings in relationship to one's own life. In sum, an **emotion** is a "dramatized feeling" that attracts or repels us to certain things because of how their specific character and qualities relates to our own fears, desires, and interests. An emotion is a kind of "feeling" because it is usually a reaction to sense perception and also is attached to feelings of pleasure or pain; but it is a "dramatized" feeling because emotions carry with them narrative

3   Richard J. Davidson, "On Emotion, Mood, and Related Affective Constructs," in *The Nature of Emotion: Fundamental Questions*, ed. Paul Ekman and Richard J. Davidson (Oxford: Oxford University Press, 1994), 51–55.

elements in which we play out scenarios in our minds of what will happen. Rhetorically, emotions are powerful tools to direct people toward or away from certain actions or judgments by connecting them to the people, objects, and events that bring about powerful responses. Emotions are therefore always objective and dramatic; they involve our active relationship with things either in the real world or in our imaginations.

Being dramatic, all emotions therefore have an orientation. An **orientation** represents how we stand in relationship to a thing, whether we are attracted to it (+) or repulsed by it (–). A *neutral* orientation in which we have no stance thus represents the absence of emotion. One can thus divide strong emotions roughly into two classifications based on positive or negative orientation. **Positive emotions** draw us closer to somebody or something; we associate such emotions with love, curiosity, pity, generosity, envy, trust, respect, obsession, or greed. Clearly, not all positive emotions are "good" ones. Sometimes we are attracted to the wrong things for the wrong reasons. The mark of a positive emotion is simply that, when something is present, people tend to want to "get closer" to it, whether to preserve it, consume it, or destroy it. **Negative emotions**, by contrast, push us negatively away from somebody or something; we associate such negative emotions with anger, fear, shame, guilt, embarrassment, anxiety, disgust, or cowardice. The characteristic response of a negative emotion is something like a "fight-or-flight" reaction in which we either try to avoid something or decide to face up to it in order to get rid of it. Of course, emotions do not always demand immediate action. Often we may love somebody and yet never talk to them, and we may be angry at those whom we must, by necessity, obey. But the lasting presence of such negative emotions usually makes us try to get out of that situation; just as positive emotions usually draw us toward something over time.[4]

If orientation indicates direction, salience represents magnitude. **Salience** represents how strongly this emotion is felt within a particular situation in the present.[5] Rhetorically, speakers typically want to increase the salience of those things they want people to consider in the present and decrease the salience of those things they believe to be irrelevant or distractions. The strategy of **amplification** increases salience by exaggerating something and making it "larger than life" so that it stands out as important and demanding of our attention. This can be done both to attract us to something and to repel us from something. For instance, nations that go to war inevitably amplify the great virtues and material rewards that will come from victory, whereas antiwar critics amplify the inevitable consequences of war. By

---

4   For a review of different perspectives on emotion, see Randolph R. Cornelius, *The Science of Emotion: Research and Tradition in the Psychology of Emotions* (Upper Saddle River, NJ: Prentice Hall, 1996).

5   For an exploration of the situational characteristic of emotional response, see Phoebe C. Ellsworth, "Some Reasons to Expect Universal Antecedents of Emotion," in *The Nature of Emotion: Fundamental Questions*, ed. Paul Ekman and Richard J. Davidson (Oxford: Oxford University Press, 1994), 150–154.

contrast, **diminution** reduces something, pushes it into the background, and makes it insignificant and trivial. To encourage attracting emotions, diminution actually seeks to reduce the level of threat in order to make something seem benign and therefore harmless.

Constructing Narratives

Given all of these characteristics of emotion, it should be clear why narrative plays such an important role in evoking pathos. The way to make people feel powerful emotions is to dramatize the role they play within a story that is connected in some way to people's lives or the things they care about. Through narrative, we situate ourselves for and against other things (orientation) and measure their importance in the present situation (salience). Strictly speaking, a **narrative** is simply a story, an account of a string of events occurring in space and time. These events do not unfold randomly, but follow an ordered series of events caused, in part, by the different purposes and actions of the characters and connected by the logic of cause and effect.

There are six essential components of any story. The **characters** are the individuals that the story is about. The **setting** is the location of the action. The **plot** is the actual story that involves the pursuit of certain goals by the characters who, after they are introduced in the exposition, must overcome obstacles. The **conflict** is what sets different characters or things at odds. The **climax** is when this conflict flares up into a decisive moment that will decide the outcome. The **resolution** is then how the conflict is resolved, whether for good or for ill. Narratives can be long and complex, like a nineteenth-century novel, or brief and condensed, like a tweet. What matters is that the audience is invited to imagine how certain characters and events interact over some period of time. In rhetorical public speaking, there are three types of narrative that stand out as particularly common and useful.

1   **Heroic narratives** describe the noble, great, and self-sacrificing actions of some individual who both strives for a virtuous ideal and overcomes great odds. We use heroic framing particularly in commemorative speeches in which we hold up certain people for praise. In telling heroic stories, the status of the person does not matter. What matters is how that person achieved great things through virtuous actions in the face of overwhelming obstacles. For instance, many families retell heroic stories of parents and grandparents who immigrated to this country with little or nothing, and yet found a way to become successful and raise a family.

2   **Tragic narratives** seek to ennoble those who suffered pain, death, or loss in pursuit of a virtuous ideal. Tragedy acknowledges that all battles cannot be won. However, tragic narratives seek to extract a broader lesson and discover a deeper wisdom even when people are grieving or sad, thus providing an opportunity for transcendence. Unlike heroic

narratives, tragic narratives do not celebrate the victories and accomplishments. Instead, they honor the virtuous lives of the actors who faced fate with character and ask us to find the wisdom in suffering.

3   **Comic narratives** describe events in which people make often ridiculous errors in judgment that result in humorous, if relatively harmless, failures. The plot of a comedy usually revolves around an initial misunderstanding or deception that magnifies to absurd proportions until some chance event reveals what is truly going on to everyone involved, such that an amicable reconciliation between parties becomes possible. Comic narratives allow us to make fun of ourselves and others for the purpose of learning from our mistakes and gaining the humility and understanding that comes with self-awareness.

The rhetorical aspect of narrative becomes clear once we are forced to choose between the validity of competing narratives about the same situation. In our interpersonal lives, we are constantly faced with this choice whenever we find ourselves caught in a dispute between mutual friends. Political situations are no different. When faced with competing narratives, an audience must decide which narrative is more "rational" to follow. Earlier we distinguished between **narrative fidelity** or how accurately a narrative represents accepted facts, and **narrative probability**, or how well the narrative holds together simply as a story, whether fictional or real. The most effective narrative from a rhetorical standpoint should have both high narrative probability *and* high narrative fidelity. Logical rationality plays a crucial role in structuring these things as well, but more often than not they begin and end in narratives whose lasting impact is usually emotional. We choose one path over another not only because it is instrumentally advantageous but because it satisfies our pride, satiates our anger, gratifies our desires, honors our family, or provides an opportunity to reward our friends and thwart our enemies.

Categories of Pathos

To make us feel something strongly about something, a rhetor must craft narratives that make this thing stand out from our general environment and endow it with particular qualities that make it worthy of our attention and concern. Rhetoric uses vivid narratives to inspire emotions that make an audience turn away from one thing and toward another. Pathos works in rhetoric, then, by dramatizing feelings and amplifying or diminishing aspects of our environment in such a way that we are actively attracted to or repelled by four categories of things—people, actions, events, and objects. **People** represent both individuals and groups (Rosa Parks, the National Academy of Sciences, the European Union); **actions** refer to conscious behavioral choices made by people (eating fast food, declaring war, philosophizing); **events** stand for time-bound, complex, moving situations that have a beginning, middle, and an end (a car accident, the Middle Ages, the

Apocalypse); and **objects** represent entities that can be understood and named as discrete things. Objects might include physical entities, real and fictional (trees, unicorns, Africa, atoms, Dante's *Inferno*, a satellite, Pluto) or conceptual objects or ideas (justice, the law of gravity, Judaism, the Bill of Rights, gay marriage).

The strategies in this chapter are therefore based on the premise that pathos is most persuasive when a speaker attaches positive or negative emotions to a specific type of "target" (a person, action, event, or object) and then amplifies that emotion through a dramatic narrative. In each of the strategies, a rhetor has embedded a person, action, event, or object and made it a central factor (for good or evil) in a dramatic narrative that has both fidelity (insofar as it reflects reality) and plausibility (insofar as it tells a good story). Combining both fidelity and plausibility within a narrative is no easy task. A narrative that has fidelity without plausibility tends to reduce to an uninspiring recounting of details, whereas a narrative that has plausibility without fidelity is interpreted as merely entertaining fiction. Only when an audience receives our stories as being both realistic and well told do they bring about the pathos that become a motive for action. It is therefore an ethical responsibility on the part of the speaker to create stories that actually represent a state of affairs and do not to slip into easy exaggeration and melodrama that play to the biases of an audience for the sake of short-term persuasive victory.

Events: Utopia and Wasteland

A narrative that focuses emotions on an event tries to create a desire for or a fear of a certain situation, happening, or outcome. Events constitute our dreams and our nightmares, our sense of what might happen in the future or may have happened in the past. Although a narrative of events inevitably discusses people, objects, and actions, those things are not the focus. Indeed, sometimes events may seem to occur unexpectedly and without any discernible cause. What matters in these narratives is the creation of desire and/or fear of those events in order to make them salient in people's minds. These narratives thus rely very heavily on vivid, graphic descriptions that make people feel as if they are in the middle of the events and experience them at that very moment. Recalling Monroe's motivated sequence, narratives of events constitute both the steps of "need" and of "satisfaction," the first being wasteland, the second, utopia.

A utopia is a vision of a perfect event, understood as a state of affairs. This event can be personal and momentary, such as the moment parents witness the birth of their first child; it can be shared and historical, such as one's memories of a golden age; and it can be shared and futuristic, such as one's visions of a promised land. In all cases, the event is portrayed as the culmination of hopes and desires that we yearn to recapture in memory or in actuality. To employ **utopia** is to use the power of an ideal to reveal the limitations of one's actual situation and inspire hope that future "perfect" events will occur. Emotions connected with utopia tend to cluster around hope, joy, patience, gratitude, and courage. If the events are inevitable, there may be joy, patience, and gratitude. If the events, however, are still in doubt, then courage and hope are produced in order to ensure that this utopian future will come to be.

The opposite of utopia is wasteland. Instead of playing on hope, it draws its power from disgust and fear produced by amplifying qualities in events that we find repulsive. Specifically, **wasteland** portrays a horrific event or state of affairs that we either wish to escape (if we are in it) or to avoid (if we are not). Whereas utopia presents a perfect state of affairs that typically has resolved all tensions, wasteland presents a state of affairs that is full of conflict and uncertainty. There are three types of situations in which wasteland is usually employed. First, wasteland can be used to motivate action by portraying one's current situation as so terrible as to be intolerable. Second, wasteland can be used to inhibit a path of action by picturing a horrible fate should one adopt the wrong path. Third, wasteland can be used to describe a past situation from which we have escaped, thereby making us content with our current lot by comparison. The first strategy motivates us to change, the second makes us fearful of change, and the third makes us content with the status quo. Wasteland emphasizes the emotions of fear, sorrow, frustration, sadness, or regret. When the wasteland that is portrayed is one's present situation, emotions that accompany it are the pain of sorrow, frustration, sadness, and regret—all of these emotions dealing with something immediately present or recently passed that we wish could be otherwise. However, when wasteland is projected into a possible future, then the primary emotion is one of fear and of a striking, visceral pain of imagining the terrifying events on the horizon.

Actions: Virtue and Vice

Whereas events are things that may happen outside of our control, actions are things that we do with conscious intent in order to make change in the world and affect the lives of ourselves and others. An action is an intervention. It redirects energies, changes courses of events, and brings about both trivial and momentous effects. To tell a narrative of actions is to show how a deliberate choice made some difference in the world that matters. However, the focus on action should emphasize the type or form of the action itself, not the character of the person who acted. For instance, the "golden rule," which tells us to "do unto others as you would have them do unto you" is an example of action because it is not about an individual person, but about a rule for behaving. Narratives of action almost always communicate some type of rule that takes the form "thou shalt" or "thou shalt not." Thus, even though the story may be about specific people or characters, as in fables or parables, the lesson of the story is about how the characters behaved and what we can learn from their choices, not whether they the actors were humans or foxes.

Virtue is employed to help us identify the nature of specific types of actions that we find worthy of praise and to generate passionate commitment to cultivating these virtues. Usually, speakers draw from numerous instances of these actions, performed by a variety of usually ordinary individuals, each of whom shows how a specific type of behavior brings about some good consequence both in practical life and in the development of character. Virtue focuses specifically on how we praise actions that arouse emotions of pride, humility, courage, guilt, and contentment. Virtue may, for instance, be used to praise the audience itself, as when a coach might praise the team for the victory by highlighting the virtues of teamwork. In this case, the emotions are of pride and contentment at achieving a level of virtue. However, rhetoric in the context of persuasion often establishes ideals of virtue by which to motivate an audience that has not yet attained them or perfected them, as for instance when a team loses and the coach instead praises the virtues of the other team. In this case, praising virtue produces a sense of humility, guilt, and courage insofar as the audience recognizes the degree to which it has failed to live up to the standards of virtue but is nonetheless committed to attain that level of excellence.

The opposite of virtue is **vice**, a strategy that repels us from certain concrete actions by making them morally offensive and/or practically harmful. Even young children are familiar with the long list of vices that they are taught to shun by reading Aesop's Fables. From "The Boy Who Cried Wolf" (lying) to "Little Red Riding Hood" (disobedience) and "The Fox and the Crow" (vanity), each of these stories is meant to attach a stigma to certain types of actions in the hope that children will avoid the temptations that often culminate in self-destructive and socially condemned behaviors. Without such a consensus about vices (alongside necessary virtues), no society could hold together for very long. And like virtue, vice is also a strategy used to guide behavior in specific rhetorical situations. In these contexts, vice usually has two functions. First, it complements virtue by telling the audience what kind of actions they should avoid if they wish to meet the challenges of the hour. Usually this list includes such devices as selfishness, vengeance, pride, impulsiveness, and the like. Second, it creates motivation through polarization by condemning the vices of an opposing group; these vices almost always include some combination of arrogance, greed, corruption, and ignorance. Combined, these two strategies justify an audience's opposition to another group while instructing them on what actions to avoid if they are not to fall into the same vices as their opponents.

People: Saint and Sinner

A narrative about a person praises or blames a specific individual (or a specific group of people acting as if they were an individual, like a team, a school, a town, or a nation) with a unique combination of qualities that makes him or her stand out as a person with a distinct and irreplaceable character. This uniqueness is what distinguishes narratives of people from narratives of action. A person may have different sets of virtues and vices, but what makes them unique is precisely this specific mix of characteristics that sets them apart from anyone else. Whereas an action can be made a rule, a person cannot. In other words, there is something "ineffable" about people that makes them impossible to ever completely define. A person embodies an infinite number of unique details and a host of contradictions that make him or her irreplaceable in the world. The narratives that focus on people, therefore, should always show how their sheer presence in a situation makes a difference, for good or for ill. That is why we buy posters featuring our favorite movie heroes and villains.

To tell a story of a **saint** is to hold up a particular person as worthy of our special attention, praise, and emulation both for its own sake as well as for our self-advancement. Rhetorically, saint is used for one of two purposes. First, saint is used to legitimate authority by creating heroic images of leaders who stand above and apart from the everyday citizenry. Second, saint can be used as a strategy to create identification by praising a particular individual with whom an audience feels a connection as well as a possibility to emulate. This strategy is common to both families and to nations. Eulogies for beloved matriarchs or patriarchs of a large family perform the same function as eulogies to heroic or noble citizens who stood for the best that a country had to offer. Those who listen to such commemorative speeches are not made to feel that sense of divine awe, often combined with fear, that is produced by praising a superhuman leader; rather, they feel a unique kinship that comes with familiarity and affection, feelings that produce in an audience a desire to emulate this person and to be as much like them as they can. To praise a saint is to make an audience feel a sense of love, charity, sympathy, pity, gratitude, or respect toward that person or group.

In **sinner**, another person (or group that we feel justified in treating as if it were an individual) is portrayed in a negative light to make that person repellent to an audience. As with saint, the key to "sinner" is to describe a person's character as possible in such a way that makes him or her stand out as particularly reprehensible (or as a reprehensible "type" of person). If the person is not described in detail, the strategy ends up becoming one of vice and becomes focused on a type of action rather than person (or type of person). There are two rhetorical functions of sinner. First, sinner undermines the legitimacy of authority by portraying the so-called "saints" in power as corrupt, cruel, and stupid. In relatively closed and oppressive societies, these rhetorical expressions often take the form of underground literature or anonymous graffiti, whereas in relatively open and democratic societies, they take the form of ubiquitous negative advertising and political harangue. Second, sinner is used for identification through polarization, creating specific images of the "not-us" so that groups know who they are fighting against and who they do not wish to become. To use narratives of sinner is to make people feel anger, shame, contempt, disgust, or hate with the aim of turning people away from certain people or lifestyles that would be corrupting and harmful.

Objects: Idol and Abomination

When we refer to objects, we refer to any identifiable and tangible part of our environment that is stable and familiar enough to label with a noun. Objects, therefore, do not simply mean discrete *physical things* such as trees and tables and pencils; they also include *organizations* such as schools and parliaments, and *processes* such as recycling and judicial review. Anything that we can define as a class of thing, with certain predictable characteristics associated with a common name, is an object. Narratives that focus on objects cannot help but drift into personification. The object takes on an active role in producing effects that can be good or bad. This often happens in television commercials quite literally. Objects become cartoon characters that speak and act, as when smiling bubbles scrub a shower door. Technology, in particular, tends to have a very active role in changing our environments, as well we purchase a smartphone, a wide screen television, a video game console, or a new SUV. But objects can also be unique and sentimental as well, for instance an old photograph or a set of military dog tags. The essential part of any narrative involving objects is to show how the objects themselves make an impact, quite apart from the choices people make or the people making those choices.

Idol is the attempt to portray an object as having such attractive qualities that an audience seeks to possess, preserve, and/or use that object. For instance, when we think of idols, we think of golden statues that possess magical forces that can be harnessed and used by the ones who possess them. The rhetorical strategy that goes by the same idol effectively is that which makes us feel this worshipful attitude toward objects. For example, ads that lead us to believe that a car will make us sexy, computers will make us powerful, energy drinks will make us athletic, and cell phones will make us worldly, all make use of idol. There are three rhetorical situations in which idol is effective. First, idol is vital to any preservationist argument that invests an object with enough *intrinsic* value that people will seek to protect it, thereby making it a crucial strategy to defend the existence of things that may not have immediate utilitarian value, including buildings, works of art, nature preserves, social organizations, and many cultural traditions. Second, idol imagines a type of perfect object that might be created by ingenuity and effort, much as one might imagine a space station on Mars. In this case, idol motivates us to action by setting forth the possibility that we might create something new in the world. Third, idol can be effectively used in rhetorical situations that require a choice from among objects that can be used as practical tools to achieve success. Idol turns our attention to specific objects and makes us feel respect, interest, surprise, curiosity, or gratitude toward them.

The opposite of idol is **abomination**, which is the attempt to make an object seem so repellent that an audience ignores, shuns, discards, or destroys it. If the idol is what gives one special power by possessing it, an abomination is something that gives one a demonic power or actively drains power away from a person. Abominations are those special classes of objects that often appear to us as benign or beneficial but in fact damage ourselves or our environment in their use. For example, cultural critics often define objects such as pop music, television, video games, pornography, and fast food as abominations that suck the life out of the young generation. Likewise, critics of political culture use abomination to categorize laws, governing bodies, corporations, political parties, or even symbols as things that impede human progress. An abomination, therefore, is not simply something that we don't like and that has distasteful qualities; it is a thing that is an active threat to our well-being and is seductive enough to warrant special condemnation. To use abomination is to make people feel disgust, fear, aversion, indifference, worry, annoyance, or hate about an object.

Conclusion

Pathos represents a form of proof that legitimates our attitudes toward objects, events, people, and actions in our environment based on how we feel about them. Although often criticized for being "irrational" forms of persuasion, pathos arguments are both unavoidable and necessary. In the first case, they are unavoidable because our language is always loaded with emotional connotations and judgments that influence the way we describe our environment. To think one can escape from pathos simply by speaking in purely technical jargon is not to leave pathos behind, but to show oneself as "apathetic," or without emotional concern. In the second case, pathos arguments are necessary because we cannot form elaborate rational judgments based on statistically good evidence about every single thing in our environment. Most of our behavior toward the people, objects, events, and actions that we encounter in our world is guided by largely emotional judgments of liking and disliking rather than true and false. Without the complex of emotional judgments about our world, we would have no background framework to make the careful logical judgments that are required in specific affairs.

We generate proofs of pathos largely by constructing narratives that show the object of interest interacting in a situation that produces an emotional response. To say that "I met an evil man yesterday" does not produce pathos simply because one labels a person with the epithet "evil." One has to show how this man interacts with his world in order for us to form an emotional judgment about him. There is a big emotional difference, for instance, between a description of a man who is poisoning a stream because he carelessly discharges wastewater from his chemical factory and a man who poisons a stream because he wishes to kill all the people in a village. We may have warrant to label both men as being "evil," but the emotions are different based on the different narratives. We may feel that the first man is evil because he is greedy and indifferent to the pain of others, whereas the second person is evil because he is cruel and inhuman. Either way, the dramatization of the *way* in which we think he is evil is what produces the emotion, not the label itself. In fact, it is often better in pathos arguments to leave the "labeling" of the emotion or characteristic to the audience. This allows them to participate in the construction of the argument without simply following the words of the speaker.

Each pair of pathos arguments generates attracting or repelling emotions to a certain type of thing. *Utopia* and *wasteland* produce emotional responses about discrete events or more enduring situations. In other words, we celebrate or condemn certain specific events in our lives, such as the moment we caught the touchdown pass or the day we heard about the death of a loved one, much in the same way that we celebrate or condemn whole eras in history, such as the Golden Age of Rome or the horrors of World War I. *Virtue* and *vice* share with utopia and wasteland a focus on activity, but these arguments emphasize the worthy or unworthiness of the action being performed by people rather than by the quality of the events produced by those actions. In virtue and vice, we either admire certain habits of action for their own intrinsic value or condemn habits of action for their complete lack of it, often regardless of the consequences. With *saint* and *sinner*, we are encouraged to respect or condemn specific people or more general types of people who can be considered collectively as an individual. For instance, politicians during the Red Scare might praise Joseph McCarthy as a saint while condemning the generic "Communist" as a sinner, therefore justifying their allegiance to McCarthy as he attempts to identify the various "sinners" in the State Department. Lastly, *idol* and *abomination* arguments perform the same function for the various "things" in our world, including not only physical things such as books and televisions but also procedural things such as laws and conceptual things like ideologies and constitutions. Idol and abomination tell us what kinds of things we should surround ourselves with in order to produce a good life and a good character.

Overall, then, the function of pathos is to make us feel like we are in a specific situation with specific types of people doing specific types of actions with specific kinds of objects. The more we can graphically dramatize the situation in which we are in, the more we feel an emotional connection to that situation and the more we are motivated to act or think in a specific way. Without emotions, we might be able to logically construct reasons for why things happen or what we should do, but these reasons are not intimately connected to us personally in a way that makes us care about them. These explanations would simply exist for us like any number of graphs or charts or line drawings or pictures. Pathos is what brings a situation to life and makes us passionate about it, focusing our reasoning and making us into agents of change. And becoming an instigator of social action is the entire purpose behind learning and mastering the art of rhetorical public speaking in a digital age.

Discussion Questions

1 We develop complex emotions very early in our development. What are some of the strongest emotional memories you can remember as a child? What type of "story" did you tell yourself as a child about what was happening?

2 When do otherwise neutral feelings suddenly take on emotional significance? Can you recall the moment when a color, smell, scent, or texture became invested with emotion?

3 Events in the news often change the way we feel about ordinary objects, particularly in times of war or national crisis. When have events on the news changed the salience and orientation of what, before, was a rather mundane object?

4 What are some of the most powerful narratives that are related by actors in a movie? The narrative can be of any quality, sentimental, terrifying, or ennobling. Find a clip of the scene and analyze why it has such an emotional power.

5 With tactics like utopia and wasteland, when is it moral (or immoral) to exaggerate future outcomes in order to motivate people to act? Does the motivation and inspiration it provides in the present have subsequent drawbacks when hopes or fears do not come to fruition?

6 Saint and sinner function to provide either role models we can imitate or villains we should shun. What are some of the most iconic saints and sinners, whether historical or fictional, that we often hear in political discourse to affect our values and goals?

7 Idol and abomination give a kind of agency and personality to objects. Do you ever feel that the mere presence of an object within a social environment determines how people interact with one another? Or does this detract from personal responsibility?

8 Virtues and vices by necessity have a somewhat abstract, law-like quality about them that speaks in generalities. But action always occurs in a unique, specific situation. To what degree do you think that our actual behavior conforms to these principles of action? Do you think that maxims like "the golden rule" actually influence our behavior?

Exercises

1 **Wonder widget**: Break into groups and have each group design and develop a new "widget"—that is, any clever mechanism or tool—to put on the market that meets some urgent need for students. Develop a sales pitch that touches on three strategies of pathos. First, praise this product as an idol that possesses intrinsic qualities and excellence, using vivid description. Second, praise the actions that one can perform with this object that make one virtuous by giving an example. Third, imagine the utopia that arises once this object becomes a part of your life.

2   **Childhood story**: Secretly assign a different ethos strategy, both positive and negative tactics, to everyone in class. Now think back on your childhood and tell a story in which a person, object, event, or action was the most important part of that story. Focus just on a single narrative that tries to get your audience to feel a specific emotion. Also, on a piece of paper, write down both the general ethos tactic as well as the specific emotion you are trying to evoke. After each story, see if the class can guess what is written on the paper.

3   **Smartphone on trial**: Divide the class into two and consider the topic of whether the object of the "smartphone" has been a net benefit or a net detriment to a happy social life and productive political culture. On each side, then subdivide each group to develop three separate argumentative strategies, the first dealing with whether or not the smartphone is an idol or abomination; the second dealing with whether the actions that we associate with smart phones are virtues or vices; the third dealing with whether culture as a whole has become a utopia or wasteland. Have each subgroup take turns presenting their arguments pro and con and take a vote at the end of class.

References

Aristotle, *On Rhetoric: A Theory of Civic Discourse*, trans. George Kennedy (Oxford: Oxford University Press, 1991).

Cooper, John M. *Reason and Emotion: Essays on Ancient Moral Psychology and Ethical Theory* (Princeton, NJ: Princeton University Press, 1999).

Cornelius, Randolph R. *The Science of Emotion: Research and Tradition in the Psychology of Emotions* (Upper Saddle River, NJ: Prentice Hall, 1996).

Davidson, Richard J. "On Emotion, Mood, and Related Affective Constructs," in *The Nature of Emotion: Fundamental Questions*, ed. Paul Ekman and Richard J. Davidson (Oxford: Oxford University Press, 1994), 51–55.

Ellsworth, Phoebe C. "Some Reasons to Expect Universal Antecedents of Emotion," in *The Nature of Emotion: Fundamental Questions*, ed. Paul Ekman and Richard J. Davidson (Oxford: Oxford University Press, 1994), 150–154.

Index

9 781032 289847